This book belongs to Anne Cahill

# Relationship Management of the Borderline Patient

## From Understanding to Treatment

# Relationship Management of the Borderline Patient

*From Understanding to Treatment*

David Dawson, M.D.
Harriet L. MacMillan, M.D.

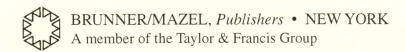
BRUNNER/MAZEL, *Publishers* • NEW YORK
A member of the Taylor & Francis Group

Library of Congress Cataloging-in-Publication Data
Dawson, David
    Relationship management of the borderline patient : from
understanding to treatment / David Dawson, Harriet L. MacMillan.
        p.      cm.
    Includes bibliographical references and index.
    ISBN 0-87630-714-4
    1. Borderline personality disorder—Treatment.   2. Psychotherapist
and patient.   I. MacMillan, Harriet L.   II. Title.
RC569.5.B67D38   1993
616.85′8520651—dc20                                              93-18886
                                                                      CIP

For information and ordering, contact:
Taylor & Francis
47 Runway Road, Suite G
Levittown, PA 19057-4700
1-800-821-8312
Manufactured in the United States of America

10   9   8   7   6   5   4

# Contents

# *Foreword*

I recall attending a symposium on Borderline Personality Disorder some time ago at an annual meeting of the American Psychiatric Association. I vaguely remember the dim auditorium and drifting between 35 millimeter slide overload and somnolence when a clinician went to the podium and began talking about no-treatment treatment of the borderline patient designed by a colleague of hers named David Dawson—or something like that. I woke up and for the first time that afternoon was sorry the presentations were limited to 20 minutes. Afterward, I found out that Dr. Dawson had been developing his no-therapy survival strategies with borderline patients for some years in Hamilton, Ontario. Later at another meeting, I had occasion to meet him briefly. I remember thinking, if not conveying, that he should write a book about his thoughts and experiences. We parted company but, happily, he fulfilled my wish and, indeed, dropped me this manuscript in the mail several years later.

I also remember several people, including Dr. Dawson himself, noting that his strategies were controversial. But I had a sense of that already, because what he presented certainly jolted me out of alpha-rhythm on that soporific afternoon. Having read his book-length elaboration, on the other hand, I find his strategies far more rational than controversial. They are to be taken seriously and represent, I think, a solid contribution to the difficult task of helping patients with Borderline Personality Disorder live with, through, and ultimately beyond their psychopathology.

I am sure that many of Dr. Dawson's ideas will strike the "traditional" therapist as iconoclastic, if not outrageous, especially if that therapist believes that the healing power of the psychotherapeutic encounter is mediated by some special interpersonal magic. Many therapists, especially those new to the craft, like to think that something qualitatively *different* occurs when one person called a therapist sits down with another person called a patient in a transaction labeled "psychotherapy." Patients with Borderline Personality Disorder are uniquely adept at demolishing such professional conceit and demonstrating that what *really* happens is quite simple and mundane, that is, two people are sitting down together to talk. If the beginning therapist is open minded and educable, he or she will get the message and accrue humility without shame. Usually, but not always, it takes the patient longer to come to the same realization, at which point the transaction has served its "therapeutic" function and can end.

It may take the patient longer to relinquish the fuzzy transitional blanket of specialness because one of the elements of Borderline Personality Disorder psychopathology is a stubborn belief that magical relations are real (at least for everyone else but themselves). At the same time, these patients possess an equally stubborn dedication to discrediting such myths. They crave magic because, at one time, it may have been the *only* answer to overwhelmingly rotten realities. They also discredit it again and again as an active repetition of what the world has done to them time and again. Although these patients are doing the best they can, their lives remain a perseverative hell, into which the accidental therapist wanders at high risk.

As long as we remain practitioners of magical psychotherapy and believe in the healing power of our own words, feelings, and personalities, the patient with Borderline Personality Disorder hoists us on our own petard and incites "countertransference" hatred and rejection in the process. Insofar as we cannot demystify what we do and accept its true everydayness, the borderline patient will keep us flat on the mat of ineffectiveness. Dr. Dawson's relationship management strategies, it seems to me, aim to do just that— demystify what we do— and do it right off the bat with the patient. When the patient begins by wondering if psychotherapy will help or whether his/her case is hopeless, etc., the answer is, "I don't know." Furthermore, the "I don't know" is not a ploy, not a manipulation, not a machiavellian maneuver. It is, simply, horribly, wonderfully, the *truth.* The therapist *does not know* the answers to these questions. Borderline personality as a disorder is too heterogeneous; the person with Borderline Personality Disorder is too complex for any kind of accurate prediction.

The course of Borderline Personality Disorder and the course of its treatment is perhaps best characterized by chaos theory, that is, outcome is sensitive to initial conditions but can't be predicted by them. This had led Michael Stone to embrace what he calls a "pragmatic" approach to treating the borderline, that is, do what you can when you can and keep your fingers crossed in between.[1] Elsewhere, I have written that the fire and rage of borderline patients needs "ice" treatment or an approach that is intermittent, continuous, and eclectic.[2]

I suspect that neither Dr. Stone's nor my treatment recommendations stir much excitement. They are too straightforward and opportunistically practical. They don't contain enough mystery or interpretive romance. Dr. Dawson's techniques are similar, although they may also be more fun. His strategies demystify the therapist, the treatment, and ultimately the patient in ways that are serious but also playful. He dares to say to the patient "I don't have all those wonderful things you have been seeking. I really don't. All I can do is spend some time talking with you. I know it doesn't seem like very much but that's all I have to offer." It is up to the patient to decide if that is good enough, at least to get going. Among those who do, a fortunate few may also come to realize that this relationship, as a prototype, can be simple, it can be fun, and it can also be remarkably free of terror.

—Thomas McGlashan, M.D.

---

[1] Stone, M. Treatment of Borderline Patients: A Pragmatic Approach. *Psychiatric Clinics of North America*, 13: 265–285, 1990.

[2] McGlashan, T.H. Implications of Outcome Research for the Treatment of Borderline Personality Disorder. In *Borderline Personality Disorder: Etiology and Treatment.* Joel Paris, ed. American Psychiatric Press, Inc., pp. 235–259, 1993.

# Preface

Many of the ideas and techniques described in this book have been fomenting in my mind for years. Their mother is necessity. Traditional (medical, psychodynamic) approaches didn't seem to help some patients. Even as a psychiatric resident some 25 years ago, I harbored the suspicion that we often made these people worse.

Over the years I experimented with different kinds of interventions, some of which, contrary to the accepted theories of the time, produced quick and dramatic changes in the behavior of those people we now call borderline. Theory followed practice and, in turn, allowed for the development of a more comprehensive and ordered system of treatment.

Dr. Harriet MacMillan added her scholarship as a clinical investigator and her experience as a child psychiatrist to the writing of this book, applied especially to the chapters on history, etiology, and adolescents. Dr. MacMillan was supported by a Travelling Fellowship from the Ontario Mental Health Foundation during the preparation of this manuscript.

Many others have contributed to the manuscript and we would like to thank all of them: the staff of 43 Charlton, the community psychiatry clinic of St. Joseph's Hospital, Hamilton, from 1975 to 1980, which at the time included Heather Munroe-Blum, who carried out many of the rudimentary formulations of relationship management. Dr. Jorge Soni, who helped hone inpatient management of borderline patients to a fine art. Drs. Rick Guscott, Paul Links, Jan Fleming, and Peter Elder for their careful reading and helpful suggestions. Dr. Jules Carbotte, Professor of Physics, for his help with Chapter 3. Dr. Giampiero Bartolucci, who, as always, clarified, connected, and expanded many of the principal author's embryonic concepts. Dr. Rod Wachsmuth for his contributions to

*xi*

the chapter on adolescents. Numerous therapists with whom we've worked and from whom we've learned in the McMaster University network of psychiatric services. And, finally, the most thanks to the many patients, clients, consumers, and survivors who have taught us that they can do much better if we give them half a chance.

D.D.

# Introduction

Sometime in my first year of residency the nurses woke me at two o'clock in the morning to ask if I would help them with a young woman who had run off the ward and was now somewhere in the neurosciences lab. We found her sitting in the corner of a room banging her head against the wall. I knelt beside her and tried to convince her that what she was doing was not constructive adult behavior, mustering as much empathy, patience, and positive regard as one can at that hour. Though she was not known to be psychotic, she ignored my entreaty and continued her activity for maybe 10 or 15 minutes. The nurses were becoming impatient with both the woman and myself. I began to consider forcible removal and chlorpromazine intramuscularly. Finally she stopped and came back to the ward with us voluntarily, but dragging her feet all the way.

On the same ward another young woman, attractive, soft, and decorative in appearance, was being seen thrice weekly by the senior resident in what we then called intensive psychotherapy. She appeared to be neither severely depressed nor psychotic. Yet one evening she sliced open the right side of her neck with a razor blade, narrowly missing the carotid artery, and badly frightening both patients and staff. She was put on heavier medication and closer observation, and the next few days we tiptoed around her (and the prominent dressing on her neck) asking ourselves if she were perhaps more depressed than she appeared (masked depression) or more psychotic than she appeared (pseudoneurotic schizophrenia).

And I began to wonder if anywhere outside a psychiatric ward, adult, intelligent people who were neither depressed nor psychotic banged their heads against the wall and cut their throats.

A year before this I had met William Dobson. He was 28, plump and sad, with a face and body that had "poor me" and "inadequate" written all over it. This being his eighth admission to the mental hospital for suicidal ideation and depression, the staff affectionately referred to him as Willy or, on occasion, Poor Willy. With drab ill-fitting shirt and pants and a slow shuffling gait, he blended into the mental hospital background.

At the time I was deeply invested in mental hospital change, therapeutic communities, and the 1960s notion that each of us will behave according to the expectations of our surroundings. So I asked that the staff begin addressing this man as Mr. Dobson and that we treat him as if he were intelligent and competent.

They had difficulty with this idea. Mr. Dobson had clearly demonstrated over the previous 10 years that he was neither intelligent nor competent. But I persisted and they eventually agreed to humor me.

Over the next 6 weeks Mr. Dobson brightened up and sharpened up (because of antidepressants the staff would say, though they had never worked before), talked with a social worker, visited the city on leaves-of-absence, found a place to live, and landed a janitorial job. I arranged his discharge for the following week.

That Saturday night the nursing supervisor called me at home to tell me that Mr. Dobson had left a suicide note and eloped. An hour later she called again to say that Mr. Dobson had phoned from a nearby tavern and wanted to talk to me. Being young and idealistic I drove 45 minutes in a snowstorm to find Mr. Dobson drinking beer with a couple of new-found friends. I joined them, bought the next round, got introduced, listened to William bemoan his life for a while, then drove him back to the hospital.

The nursing staff had expected this relapse: His show of health had been an illusion, or a "flight into health," according to the local psychoanalyst. Nonetheless, ignoring their feeling that he wasn't ready and William's predictions of self-destruction, I crossed my fingers and discharged him. He kept the janitorial job and I saw him as an outpatient, twice blocking readmissions when he visited the general hospital emergency department threatening suicide, but finally failing to prevent a readmission when he confessed to the emergency physician that he was suffering from an overwhelming impulse to sexually abuse small children.

This was probably the first, but certainly not the last time I questioned the concept of "inadequate personality." Inadequate Mr. Dobson always left behind a battlefield strewn with the bodies of failed professional helpers.

Another young woman, slight and blonde, transformed herself day to day from a vacant-eyed waif with numerous fantasies and strange perceptions, to a darkly eye-shadowed seductress, to a suicidally depressed maniac, to a tough, masculinized gay. She had been in treatment since her first overdose at age 16, repeating her story over the years, of her father molesting her when she was only 2, her breath-holding through her childhood, the gang rape at 14, her numerous escapades with men of all ages and persuasions, her drug taking, overdoses, wrist cutting, living in a commune on Fourth Avenue, and her ongoing battle with her mother, who wore frilly white blouses and read psychology books in an attempt to understand her daughter.

On this, her first admission to a provincial mental hospital but her seventh to a psychiatric ward, we gave her individual and group psychotherapy, treated her anxiety, treated her depression, treated her conflict with her mother, and even tried to treat her psychotic tendencies. But she continued to act badly, alone or in league with a young male. When the staff found her in bed, first with a very sick and pathetic young man and then with a rough psychotic cowboy, they were in turn furious with her and protective of her.

She broke windows and cut her wrists. In the seclusion room she went on a hunger strike. Most males she came in contact with wanted to rescue her. The females were more prudent. We tried sleep therapy in the form of bed rest and heavy sedation for a 7-day period, thinking, I suppose, that if we could only slow the thermodynamic turmoil of her brain cells they might reorganize themselves in a more reasonable fashion. But 7 days later she was unchanged in her changeableness, once again adopting various personae, as if absorbing the ghosts of the institution.

I transferred to a newly built psychiatry ward on the university campus and took her with me. I still had faith in the Poor Willy/Mr. Dobson transformation and instructed the new and eager staff that we would treat this young woman as if she were a sane, competent, responsible, adult person. This worked well for a month or so until some passing hippies whisked her back to Fourth Avenue. Over the next 10 years she bounced in and out of therapy, confusing and frustrating therapists of numerous disciplines and theoretical persuasions.

At the time, however, I was beginning to wonder if the problem, at least with this group of patients, lay within the institution of psychiatry, rather than within the patient. Somehow, in our attempts to contain, nurture, protect, and treat these disordered young people, we were contributing to, maybe even causing, their more outrageous and dangerous behavior.

Another young woman on the same ward, Ann, repeatedly over a 3 month period proclaimed the desire to kill herself. Fortunately this ward did not have lockable doors or seclusion rooms, and so we had no effective way of preventing her from killing herself. On the other hand, because of her suicide threats we could not discharge her. The impasse finally ended when she withdrew her decision to commit suicide and signed herself out. I wondered, at the time, if there were any social context outside a psychiatric ward where someone might threaten suicide, continually, daily, and be asked about it daily, for a 3-month period.

I had been treating Betty for 2 months, quite successfully I thought, when she informed me that she was still suicidal and still planned to kill herself, but that since she liked and respected me she would not do it until I had left for my year in England. She was keeping herself alive for my sake. I left for England and later heard that she had unsuccessfully overdosed a few days after my departure.

On a medium-stay ward in an English mental hospital, a young woman threatened to jump out the second-story window unless she received the same treatment she had been given twice before, electroconvulsive therapy, or ECT. When the staff had tired of constant observation and periodically pulling her back from the window, I arranged with the anesthetist to conduct a placebo ECT.

At first the anesthetist resisted, suggesting that although I could order proper ECT, a higher authority was needed for placebo ECT. But he finally agreed and we went through with it, giving her preanesthesia, induction, oxygen, everything except electricity. Over the next 2 days she made a remarkable recovery.

A senior resident, generally disdainful of any thought or activity not purely biological, was gamely attempting psychotherapy with a difficult, angry, impulsive woman in her mid-twenties. For several years she had been in and out of the hospital and various psychotherapy relationships, was unemployed, and looked to be making a career of psychiatric problems. One afternoon, in the middle of a session, the resident lost his temper, jumped up from his chair and shouted at her, "You are completely hopeless. You have a severe untreatable personality disorder. You will never get better. There's no point in my seeing you any longer." The woman stormed out of the room, caught a bus downtown, got herself a job, and was not seen near psychiatry over the next 2 years.

A single man, living in hotel rooms, addicted to Demerol, was coming to see me as an outpatient. I refused to give him drugs. He displayed many signs of stress and distress. He was also threatening to jump off of a nearby bridge. This posed a dilemma. I knew he should not be hospitalized, that it would do him no good in the long run, but he was registered as an outpatient of the hospital and so should he jump (and I thought it possible), there would be an inquest and I would have to explain to my supervisor, the head of the department, the administrator of the hospital, the coroner, the hospital lawyer, and, in my imagination, a newspaper reporter, why I had not hospitalized a man so sick and desperate. The simple solution was to stop seeing him. But I was young and sought a more humanitarian way around this problem. I officially discharged him, closed the file on him, but kept seeing him. Now, should he jump, it would be a private matter between him and me. I was then able to say to him something like, "I don't want you to kill yourself, but I have no way of stopping you if that is truly what you wish to do. It's entirely up to you. Meanwhile I'll continue seeing you weekly."

All right. The problem is not entirely psychiatry's. These people do have something wrong with them—something wrong inside their heads, their psyches or their personalities. But I was beginning to understand that only in their relationships with psychiatry and medicine were their worst potentials realized.

In 1969, despite the teachings of George Herbert Mead, Harry Stack Sullivan, and Erving Goffman, psychoanalytic and biological thinking so predominated that we had no way of conceptualizing the problem as something that lay between the patient and the therapist, or in the distorted relationships these particular patients develop with psychiatric institutions. Transference and countertransference could be invoked, but beyond allowing an interpretation of the patient's behavior, did not substantively change either the relationship or the usual poor outcome. Systems theory became popular but we used it to understand family systems rather than the patient's/family's relationship with the institution.

So I began to search for a new way of understanding these patients and our relationship with them—a concept that would offer some specific and practical management techniques, methods of managing them that would *not* "make them worse before they got better" (a somewhat self-serving aphorism popular at the time) and not lead to the more outrageous self-destructive behavior that seems to occur when and only when they are in the hospital or in a traditional therapeutic relationship.

The result of this search is what I have been calling *relationship managements*, which I hope is adequately and helpfully explained in the succeeding chapters of this book.

Chapter 1 offers a short history of the borderline concept, tracking the convoluted semantic shift from something that is an extension of something else, to independent status, and notes the influence of time and place on our perceptions and explanations.

Chapter 2 discusses the literature on etiology and reflects on the manner in which an adult borderline self-system might be engendered by the experiences of an abused child.

The language of etiology and of common therapies reflects a belief in objective observation, independent entities, and linear cause-effect mechanisms. A conceptual shift may be required to fully appreciate and manage the behaviors of those people psychiatrists call borderline. Chapter 3 explains this.

Chapter 4 describes the self-system of the borderline client and the context in which he or she resides, and the manner in which these two contructs are interdependent. This formulation provides the theoretical base for all that follows.

Chapter 5 outlines the principles of relationship management. These principles are applied in crisis management in Chapter 6, in inpatient management in Chapter 7, and in outpatient or office management in Chapter 8.

Chapter 9 explains the modifications that need to be considered when applying this model to borderline behavior in adolescents.

Relationship management techniques may be very helpful in the treatment of people with other kinds of personality disorder. Chapter 10 contains a few examples of this.

There are many clinical situations in which clients do not have borderline personality disorders, and may have DSM-III-R axis I diagnoses, but who nevertheless benefit from the application of some of the principles and techniques illustrated in this book. Chapter 11 portrays specific circumstances in which relationship management can be applied to some of the difficulties people with schizophrenia present to wards and clinics.

There are some dangers in the unbridled and/or unsophisticated application of relationship management. Chapter 12 explores some of these situations.

Finally, four case studies are presented in Chapter 13 in a manner, we hope, that illustrates the shift in concepts, language, and attention needed to arrive at simple and effective relationship management of difficult borderline patients.

In several chapters in this book clinical vignettes are presented that might not satisfy current criteria for the diagnosis of borderline personality disorder. We are not blushing about this for several reasons. First, the criteria are not static; they shift with changes in theory, professional interest, culture, and scientific study. Second, as discussed in several chapters, notably Chapter 3, the very search for, and application of, seemingly objective criteria is conceptually limiting. And in so far as a belief in objective observation and non-prejudicial labeling is part of the language of the traditional social contract of the medical model, it can contribute to iatrogenic disability. As our patients prove to us over and over again, all may not be as we first perceive it.

But more importantly the concepts and techniques described in this book are most effective when applied in clinical situations where the behavior being observed or addressed is being driven primarily by interpersonal imperatives. Those people who, by any of the current criteria, tend to be labeled borderline fall squarely in this category. But not exclusively and possibly not inclusively.

The principal author has been developing and using these ideas for 20 years. A controlled study of the application of these techniques to the group treatment of borderline patients is currently being completed. Otherwise they have not, as yet, undergone the rigors of scientific outcome studies. But over these years the authors, their students, and supervisees have found them broadly helpful and often dramatically effective.

One clinical vignette is presented later in which a notoriously difficult and chaotic patient becomes a stable mental health worker after the application of relationship management. This is not an isolated case.

At first glance the concepts and especially the techniques espoused seem simple enough. They are not. Therapists often find them counterintuitive, and certainly counter to all those impulses that led to such a career choice in the first place. Some of the recommendations also run counter to training. It is difficult to apply them in isolation, without at least peer consultation.

I find it much easier to consult on and supervise others using these techniques than to apply them myself, at least consistently over a period of time. Just when I feel good about dramatic changes in a couple of clients, brought about by masterly use of relationship management, another client will come along and tie me in knots.

It is also possible for some therapists to learn the words without the music. As a therapist once said to me, "I used your model. I told him he would have to be responsible for himself." Well, she didn't quite get the idea, and in not quite getting the idea, assumed the very position she should have been avoiding. Her phrase "I told him he would have to" contravenes the phrase, "responsible for himself," interpersonally speaking. Her tone and prosody probably betrayed her as well. Undoubtedly, the distorted interpersonal negotiations simply moved to a different plane.

This last paragraph might not be meaningful to a reader who started at the beginning of this book. I hope it will be later. The point here is that full value of the concepts and techniques of relationship management might come gradually, after reading, practicing, experimenting, re-reading, discussion, and supervision.

There is a lot of internal work that needs to be done for the successful application of techniques that, at first glance, seem simple and concrete. They must also be adjusted to fit, to integrate with, the skill sets and basic personality of each different therapist. Some of us find it easier to respond slowly than do others. Some of us find it very difficult to withhold what we at the time perceive as help, support, kindness, and professional responsibility. And some of us find it very difficult not to display what we at the time experience as wisdom, intellect, and expertise.

With these few caveats then, this book is offered to therapists of all disciplines with the hope that the contents therein, when fully digested and adapted, will make your work less stressful and improve the lives of those people we know are your most troubling and difficult clients.

D.D.

". . . this whole world is only object in relation to subject, perception of a perceiver, in a word, idea."

—Arthur Schopenhauer

"What is interesting about logical thought . . . is that once having been mastered, its rules master us."

—Robert Heilbroner

# Part I
## History, Etiology, Concepts

# 1

## History of the Borderline Concept

Several years ago, as a resident in psychiatry, I (H.M.) was asked to see a very disruptive woman on the hematology service. "She is interfering with the functioning of the ward and we can't control her behavior," complained the nurses and the hematologist. "She's always threatening suicide."

In my consultation with the hematologist, I tried to explain the patient's behavior and recommend management strategies. He listened politely but remained unsatisfied. He wanted a psychiatric diagnosis. Reluctantly, I suggested that the patient had a borderline personality disorder.

"Borderline," he shouted. "Even I can tell she has a definite personality disorder!"

The concept borderline personality disorder differs from other diagnoses in medicine where the term "borderline" is applied. In most medical specialties borderline means almost, on the edge, not full-blown, or not quite satisfying the criteria, reflecting a model of continuity. The *Oxford Dictionary* defines borderline as "a boundary strip of land" and "verging on the indecent, insanity," staying within a continuity paradigm. In today's North American psychiatry the word borderline is used to name a distinct (if still controversial) category, reflecting the current supremacy of discontinuous models. It has taken 80 years to arrive at our present semantic contradiction.

Discontinuous and continuous models have always competed for our attention. Responding to a practical and perhaps biological

*3*

need to categorize, we label, define, redefine, and package clusters of symptoms and traits, only to find our satisfaction short-lived. Someone working in a different context perceives these clusters differently, and patients or clients appear who don't quite fit. We are then forced to consider a continuous model, or spectrum, and perhaps use the term borderline, but this implies that these patients who don't quite fit are somehow related to the patients in the main category. This relationship, in turn, might be one of *kind* (overlap of symptoms, family histories, or inferred psychic structures or dynamics), or of *course* (similar prognosis and outcome), or of *transition* (the borderline patients will eventually satisfy the criteria of the main category), or of *response to treatment.*

It is hardly surprising that the term borderline would be ambiguous to a clinician outside the field of psychiatry when there has been, and perhaps still is, such confusion about the concept within the psychiatric literature (Aronson, 1985). "Few diagnoses in psychiatry currently attract more attention and controversy than the borderline conditions . . ." (Reiser & Levenson, 1984, p. 1528). Despite this controversy, the term borderline has come to refer to a relatively distinct group of clients who are not bordering on something else. This was not always the case.

Kraepelin wrote about atypical or "borderland" cases of schizophrenia (Tarnopolsky & Berelowitz, 1984). He recognized that there existed certain states between insanity and normality (Mack, 1975). As psychoanalytic concepts gained acceptance the borderline patient was thought by one group to have a mild form of schizophrenia, and by a second group, to have a disorder on the continuum between neurosis and psychosis (Goldstein, 1987).

The first group of authors applied the concept of borderline schizophrenia to patients with schizophrenic traits without obvious schizophrenia (Stone, 1980). Zilboorg (1941) used the term "ambulatory schizophrenia"; Hoch and Polatin (1949) focused on a group of patients who resembled neurotics but exhibited more pervasive anxiety and symptoms of thought disturbance, using the rather excessive label pseudoneurotic schizophrenia. The second group of authors focused on the borderline concept as a distinct syndrome within the realm of neurosis and psychosis (Goldstein, 1987; McGlashan, 1983).

Stern (1938) was the first to use the term borderline to distinguish a group of apparently neurotic patients who worsened while undergoing psychoanalysis. He concentrated on a group of patients who had no overt signs of psychosis but who manifested low self-esteem and an infantile defensive organization (Mack, 1975). Stern, as other psychoanalysts, focused on the underlying psychic conflicts of such disorders.

In 1942, Helene Deutsch introduced the concept of the "as if personality." These patients had disturbed relationships, had a lack of identity, and were "fixed" at an early level of development. They appeared socially appropriate but in fact had very disturbed relationships (Gunderson & Singer, 1975).

The term borderline, representing a separate entity, really became popularized by Robert Knight in 1953. Knight was among the first psychoanalysts to clearly separate the borderline condition from the realm of schizophrenia (Akiskal, 1981). Knight described disturbances of object relationships and weakened ego functions as characteristics of the borderline patient. He believed that borderline patients exhibited similarities to both neurotic and psychotic patients (Goldstein, 1987). It was following the publication of two papers by Knight in 1953 that the American Psychoanalytic Association first recognized the concept borderline by holding two panels about this disorder (Mack, 1975).

In 1959, Schmideberg wrote about the borderline patient as being not only quantitatively apart from both neurotic and psychotic individuals but also qualitatively different. She perceived the borderline syndrome as an enduring life-long pattern with severe personality disturbance, and is often quoted for her description of the borderline patient as being "stable in his instability" (Aarkrog, 1981).

By the 1950s, psychoanalysis had become divided into various theoretical groups. Authors such as Stern and Schmideberg were representative of the movement away from any association between schizophrenia and borderline (Stone, 1981). In 1966, Kernberg presented a description of the psychostructural concept of "borderline personality organization" (1967). He considered this group of patients to occupy a position between neurosis and psychosis but saw this position as a stable, pathological organization rather than as a fluctuating state. Much of Kernberg's work was based on the object-relations theories of Melanie Klein, Ronald Fairbairn and Donald Winnicott (Mack, 1975). Kernberg has emphasized the defensive functioning of individuals with borderline personality organization, particularly the defense mechanism of "splitting."

Kernberg wrote about the confusion in the literature surrounding the term borderline. He objected to the term "state" because it implied a transitory, fluctuating constellation of symptoms. Kernberg and colleagues (1981) postulated that borderline personality organization can be distinguished from neurotic and psychotic levels of organization through use of three structural criteria: "degree of identity integration, level of defensive operations, and capacity for reality testing" (page 225).

In the book *The Borderline Syndrome: A Behavioral Study of Ego-Functions*, Grinker and colleagues (1968) remarked about the lack of systematic empirical research on the borderline concept. They also noted that the main body of works had come from psychoanalysts rather than general psychiatrists. Grinker's group was the first to investigate several hypotheses put forth about the borderline patient. The following four subcategories were described using the technique of cluster analysis (Aarkrog, 1981; Lonie, 1985):

1. A severely disturbed group bordering on the psychotic
2. A core borderline group with negative affect and acting-out behavior
3. "As if" persons with poor sense of self
4. A less severely disturbed group with neurotic features

Grinker set out to define the borderline syndrome and described behavior according to an ego-psychology framework. He identified four characteristics common to all categories: (a) anger as the main affect; (b) defect in affectional relationships; (c) lack of self-identity; and (d) depressive loneliness (Grinker et al., 1968).

In 1975, Gunderson and Singer reviewed the descriptive literature on borderline patients. They noted the numerous terms that had been associated with borderline, including "patient, state, personality organization, character, pattern, schizophrenia, condition or syndrome"(p. 1). They emphasized that the description of borderline cases is influenced by the context in which patients are observed and by methods of sample selection and data collection. A set of operational criteria was developed that included (a) intense affect; (b) history of impulsive behavior; (c) social adaptiveness; (d) brief psychotic experiences; (e) bizarre performance on psychological testing; and (f) chaotic interpersonal relationships. This review served to narrow the definition of borderline personality disorder.

Despite a growing trend to consider the borderline syndrome as a distinct clinical entity during the late 1960s and early 1970s, the term "borderline schizophrenia" was used in 1968 by Kety and associates. This syndrome was discussed in their adoptive studies that examined the contribution of nature and nurture in schizophrenia (Kety et al., 1968). In 1978, Gunderson and Kolb compared borderline patients with schizophrenic patients as well as other groups. The patients were interviewed using the Diagnostic Interview for Borderlines (DIB), which is a semistructured interview developed for the identification of borderline personality disorder (Kolb & Gunderson, 1980). It was concluded from this work that borderline patients could be discriminated from other groups, including schizophrenic patients.

Spitzer et al., in 1979, emphasized again the ongoing confusion about the definition of the borderline concept in their description of the disagreement among the members of the American Psychiatric Association Task Force on Nomenclature and Statistics: "Their attitudes reflect the divided opinions within our profession. Some believed that the borderline concept represents everything that is wrong with American psychiatry . . . Others believed that there is sufficient evidence of the utility of one or more of these concepts to warrant their inclusion . . ." (Spitzer et al., 1979, p. 17).

This was a time of heightened controversy around the borderline concept. Rich, in 1978, was critical of the use of the word borderline, and advocated dropping it from psychiatric nosology. He recommended considering these patients as "undiagnosed," which was based on recommendations by Hudgens (1971). In reviewing the evidence for the reliability and validity of the borderline concept, Perry and Klerman (1978, p. 141) performed a comparative analysis of four sets of criteria: the "borderline states" of Knight, the "borderline personality organization" of Kernberg, the "borderline syndrome" of Grinker et al., and the "borderline patients" of Gunderson and Singer. Perry and Klerman (1978) reported on the striking differences among criteria proposed by the various authors. They stated, "In one way or another, it seems as if the whole range of psychopathology of personality is represented" (p. 150). The authors proposed a "moratorium on further general clinical descriptive and psychodynamic papers on the borderline patient" (p. 148).

It was amidst this controversy, that Spitzer and colleagues, with the American Psychiatric Association Task Force on Nomenclature and Statistics, set out to develop criteria for the two major uses of the term borderline (Spitzer et al., 1979). The concept of borderline schizophrenia was represented by the word "schizotypal," and the term "unstable personality" was chosen to represent the concept of borderline personality.

The term unstable personality was not accepted, however, as it was argued that the borderline personality demonstrates "stable instability." It was following this work that distinct diagnostic categories were created in the third edition of the *Diagnostic and Statistical Manual of Mental Disorders* (DSM-III): schizotypal personality disorder and borderline personality disorder (American Psychiatric Association, 1980).

The term "schizotypal personality disorder" as outlined by Spitzer et al. (1979) included criteria that were closely related to previous concepts of borderline schizophrenia. The diagnostic grouping "borderline personality disorder" was characterized by impulsivity, identity disturbance, self-destructive acts, affective instability, and feelings of emptiness.

Following the inclusion of borderline personality disorder in DSM-III, the search intensified for a description of a borderline concept that was valid and reliable. Although the term borderline originated with clinically oriented psychoanalysts, the concept had been further developed by researchers and was by this time receiving attention from general psychiatrists (Stone, 1981).

In the early 1980s, there was a further shift away from consideration of borderline in the schizophrenic realm, with emphasis on borderline as a subaffective disorder (Akiskal, 1981). Although work continued on establishing guidelines for the diagnosis of borderline personality disorder, several researchers turned their attention to examination of the association between borderline personality disorder and affective disorder. In 1981, Akiskal reviewed the evidence for this association and described his series of borderline patients, many of whom had some form of affective disorder. In the same year, Liebowitz and Klein (1981) published a paper examining the relationship between borderline personality disorder and hysteroid dysphoria. They emphasized the importance of sorting out those borderline characteristics that are affective in nature—specifically those symptoms that show drug responsivity. The search for subtypes of the borderline concept was fueled at this time by mounting interest in pharmacological treatment.

In 1981, Groves wrote about borderline personality disorder in the *New England Journal of Medicine*. Up until this time, interest in this condition had been confined mainly to the psychiatric profession, although increasingly other clinicians had begun looking at their difficult patients through the same set of conceptual prisms. As recently as 1986, an article appeared in the *Lancet* with the statement, "Although it is possible to get agreement between psychiatrists as to what constitutes a borderline personality, the concept remains diffuse and the label is in danger of overuse" ("Management of Borderline Personality Disorders," 1986, p. 847).

Despite the popular use of the term borderline in North America, British psychiatrists, as one might expect, have been more skeptical (Tarnopolsky & Berelowitz, 1987). In 1982, an article appeared in the *Archives of General Psychiatry* entitled "Are There Borderlines in Britain?" (Kroll et al., 1982). The authors set out to examine whether there existed a population of patients that met the DSM-III criteria for borderline personality disorders, and if so, what the differences were in the clinical picture of British and American borderline patients. They concluded that there does exist a group of patients in Britain who fit the borderline description but that these patients reported only minimal drug abuse and no drug-related psychoses. British psychiatrists diagnose these patients according to ICD-9 (World Health Organization, 1978) as having personality disorders, but differentiation of borderline from other types of personality disorders has not yet been established.

A study done at the Maudsley Hospital in Britain showed that approximately 25% of the psychiatrists at that institution use the diagnosis of "borderline personality" (Tarnopolsky & Berelowitz, 1984). This finding was similar to that of Macaskill and Macaskill (1981, 1985), who explored usage by Scottish psychiatrists. It is of note that all of the consultants in the Maudsley Hospital sample who described themselves as psychoanalytically oriented made use of the term borderline.

Although much of the research into the borderline concept during the 1980s was focused on clarification and compartmentalization, the psychoanalytically oriented psychiatrists conducted research into the intrapsychic organization of their patients, including defensive structure. Kernberg developed a structural interview involving four techniques: (a) clarification; (b) confrontation; (c) interpretation, and (d) transference interpretation (Kernberg et al., 1981). Lerner and colleagues (1981) compared the defensive functioning of borderline patients and schizophrenic patients on the Rorschach and concluded that borderline patients exhibit a defensive organization that can be distinguished from that of patients with schizophrenia.

Greene and colleagues (1986) have remarked on the imbalance that exists between diagnosis-related and treatment-oriented research. They advocate a shift away from the diagnostic area toward the study of psychotherapeutic issues that arise in the treatment of borderline patients.

In a recent discussion of the treatment of these patients, Silver (1985) has used the phrase "characterologically difficult." He emphasizes the heterogeneity of this population, and focuses on general treatment principles of this diverse group. While the search continues for the ideal categorization of the borderline phenomenon, authors such as Silver advocate a shift toward the understanding of relationship patterns in these patients. Reiser and Levenson (1984) point out the danger of clinicians using the term borderline as a form of "pseudoscientific jargon." "Borderline" is also used pejoratively in many clinics and wards, and more than one clinician has pointed out a possible sexist underpinning to the concept.

This brings us to the current dilemma: the struggle to define and categorize the borderline concept in a way that allows meaningful research, without the loss of theoretical understanding and clinical usefulness.

It is very clear from this history that we suffer from a strong need to categorize the people we meet in our offices and hospitals. This is, in essence, the application of the disease model, and it is certainly true that the discovery of effective treatment is greatly abetted by the successful (reliable and valid) description of a syndrome. But it is also clear from this history that our descriptions of these particular clients have been very context bound. The psychoanalysts, working in office practices, and thinking in terms of inferred psychic mechanisms (rather than observable traits) on a continuum from neurotic to psychotic organization, described their borderline patients accordingly. These borderline patients came to their notice because they did not respond well to psychoanalysis.

The hospital psychiatrists, working with a population that included major psychoses, found some patients who gave them as much trouble as schizophrenics but who did not exhibit a full range of psychotic symptoms. When it was popular to consider psychopathology as a continuous spectrum, these patients were categorized as borderline schizophrenic. When European influences pushed our concept of schizophrenia into that of a more specific if not always clear-cut disease, the borderline group became detached. With the advent of lithium, the borderline category was partially engulfed by the expanding concept and diagnosis of major affective disorder.

Attempts to define, categorize, and subcategorize these particular patients will continue. In the meantime, physicians and other professional helpers still have a very difficult client group to deal with. Our attempts to categorize and describe these people have been field dependent or context bound, that is, bound to institutional imperatives, current technologies, national and professional cultures, traditional social contracts, and fashionable conceptual models. Our difficulties helping them may arise from the very same influences.

# 2

# Notes on Etiology

The problems encountered in defining the concept "borderline" as discussed in Chapter 1 contribute to the complexity of examining etiologic factors as well. A theoretician writing in 1970 may be addressing a different population than an empiricist writing in 1993. And while many theorists have provided us with important ways of understanding borderline pathology (Segal, 1988), it is necessary to distinguish between theoretical concepts and empirical evidence for etiologic links. As the epidemiologists tell us, evidence for a causal link requires that three criteria be met: (a) there must be an association between a variable and the disorder; (b) the occurrence of the variable must antedate the disorder, and (c) there must be evidence that the variable has a causal role in the disorder (Department of Clinical Epidemiology and Biostatistics, 1981). A host of ideas has arisen to explain the phenomena observed in the treatment of borderline patients, but as Westen (1990) states: . . . "the number of theories postulating various stages and structures continues to proliferate, and clinical data and methods have proven inadequate for distinguishing good theories from bad or better ones" (p. 661).

Several recent reviews address the etiology of borderline disorder among children Petti & Vela, 1989; (Robson, 1991; Meijer & Treffers, 1991), but the focus of this chapter is confined to adults and adolescents.

The object-relations theorists point to the early mother-child relationship. The role of the father in shaping the personality structure of the infant, not surprisingly, has been largely ignored (Segal, 1988). Much of the early work is based on Mahler and colleagues'

(1975) writings about the psychological birth of the infant, referred to as the separation-individuation process. This process includes three phases of development ultimately resulting in the child's attaining "a sense of self and of separateness distinct from the mother" (Rinsley, 1980, p. 127). The rapprochement subphase of separation-individuation is a time of the child's growing realization of being separate from the mother (16–25 months). The core conflict at this stage is between the child's drive for independence and mastery and the child's need for a state of symbiosis with the mother (Rinsley, 1980; Wong, 1980). As summarized by Wong (1980), with "good enough mothering" (a concept from Winnicott, 1955) the rapprochement crisis is resolved and the child can "move on to the fourth subphase to achieve individuality and object constancy" (p. 108).

Several authors have focused on this rapprochement subphase as the point at which "fixation" can result in a psychic structure that will later emanate borderline symptomatology (Mahler, 1972; Masterson & Rinsley, 1975). According to Kernberg's developmental stages, fixation resulting in borderline personality development occurs between 4 and 12 months of age (Kernberg, 1972; Masterson & Rinsley, 1975). However, Kernberg doesn't blame the mother. He attributes the failure of the infant to develop an integrated self-concept to constitutional factors (Kernberg, 1966; Masterson & Rinsley, 1975). He refers to the child's lack of anxiety tolerance as an example. Kernberg also suggests that this developmental failure results in a lingering dissociation between good and bad self and object representations (Masterson & Rinsley, 1975). On the other hand, Masterson and Rinsley emphasize the mother's role in causing the developmental failure that results in borderline symptomatology through adolescence and adulthood. The mother, they say, clings to her infant in response to the child's tentative steps toward individuation. They refer to the mother as "herself suffering from a borderline syndrome" (1975, p. 167), a statement that has not been confirmed through empirical work (Meijer & Treffers, 1991; Singer, 1977; Shapiro, 1978).

In 1981 Masterson revised this original theory stating, "contribution to the etiology may come from either or both sides of the mother-child equation" (p. 132). He continued to emphasize however that the central issue in the development of borderline pathology was "the mother's unavailability for the child's separation-individuation needs" (p. 132).

Kernberg (1967) and Masterson and Rinsley (1975) have emphasized the use of splitting as a mechanism of defense by the ego of the borderline. All three authors also agree on developmental failure in separation-individuation as the cause of the borderline personality (Soloff & Millward, 1983). Soloff and Millward refer to this theoretical framework as the separation hypothesis and emphasize the common theme of early-life deprivation. This deprivation may have many causes, but their focus is on circumstances that disturb the mother-child relationship. Similarly, Buie and Adler (1982–83) think the borderline personality results from a failure to develop sufficient resources for "holding-soothing" required independently later in life. They emphasize that the normal child, having little capacity for this ability, must rely on "good enough" mothering for it. Inadequate mothering may range from intentional neglect to unavoidable separations.

Masterson and Rinsley (1975) point out that the evidence for their theory focusing on the role of the mother in the genesis of the borderline personality derived from observation and treatment of borderline mothers and borderline adolescents, that is, people who are patients interacting with helpers within a very specific social context. As cited by Wong (1980), Grinker and Werble (1977) have questioned the methodology of the information arising from the psychoanalytic literature. They point out that there is seldom sufficient information regarding the methodological details of these investigations.

As elegant and satisfying as some of these theories may be, they all deserve empirical testing and reevaluation in light of ongoing research. For example, if one holds firmly to Masterson and Rinsley's theory that an individual with a borderline personality often results from a mother with the same syndrome, this could have, in theory, far-reaching implications for treatment and prevention. And does this relationship hold for 100%, 50%, or 30% of borderline patients? A corollary for which we have more accurate data is that although it is important to know that approximately 30% of children who experience physical abuse will go on to abuse their own offspring, it is equally important to understand that the majority of individuals will not (Kaufman & Zigler, 1987). What are the differentiating factors?

In a recent review, Westen (1990) examines ways in which systematic research on object relations in borderline patients can provide important theoretical information. He challenges several of the assumptions related to the origin of character pathology such as borderline personality disorder. For example, he states that one assumption of object-relations theories is that "the origin of severe character pathology lies in the first three years of life, in the relation between infant and mother" (p. 664). Westen points out that etiologic influences related to specific phases are difficult to evaluate because generally the same child and caretakers interact beyond the specific period under consideration. He makes the point that we do not know that "good enough" parenting during later childhood years could not alter the early features of borderline personality disorder. Westen also poses the question as to whether clinical observation resulting from the treatment of pathological individuals is sufficient for the development of object-relations theories.

Clinicians may find specific theories fit specific patients very neatly. The ensuing formulation of the pathogenesis of that patient's problems may almost write itself, and be very helpful in developing treatment strategies. But this process, the application of etiologic theories to the problems of the patient sitting opposite the therapist, as necessary and helpful as it might be in psychological treatment, is quite distinct from two other phenomena: the reality, the dynamics, and the problems of the here-and-now relationship between patient and therapist, and a true, proved, linear cause-effect relationship.

When discussing the pathogenesis of borderline conditions, Egan (1988) emphasizes two main categories: one with developmental origins as discussed above and another he terms "biologic." He cites the work of Stone as supporting the view that biological factors are significant in the etiology of borderline conditions (Stone, 1980). Stone (1981) has expressed the view that borderline conditions resemble versions of mood disorders, which have strong biological aspects. Both Stone (1979) and Akiskal (1981) have emphasized the high prevalence of mood disorders among family members of borderline patients. Davis and Akiskal (1986) have summarized the biological aspects of borderline personality disorder. They highlight the relationship of bipolar and unipolar illness to the borderline condition. These authors cite the study by Loranger et al. (1982) as further evidence of the familial-genetic links of the disorder. Loranger and colleagues examined borderline symptomatology among relatives of borderline patients compared to that among relatives of patients with schizophrenia and bipolar disease. The relatives of patients with borderline symptoms were much more likely to have been treated for "borderline or borderline-like disorder" than were the relatives of the comparison patients. In a study of same-sex borderline twins, genetic factors were not found to affect the development of borderline personality disorder (Torgersen, 1984); however, the prevalence of this disorder was low in the sample, limiting detection of this finding (Links, 1991). Davis and Akiskal conclude that pedigree studies strengthen the theory that borderline conditions are subtypes of mood disorder.

Several authors point to the similarities between attention-deficit hyperactivity disorder and borderline conditions, including impulsivity, low frustration tolerance, lability of affect and tendency towards substance abuse and antisocial behavior (Soloff & Millward, 1983; Egan, 1988). An association has been hypothesized between central nervous system impairment in childhood and borderline personality disorder in adulthood (Soloff & Millward, 1983). As summarized by Gardner and colleagues (1987), investigations of neurophysiological dysfunction among borderline patients have revealed abnormal electroencephalogram results (Cowdry et al., 1985–86), history of CNS insults (Andrulonis et al., 1981), and a greater number of neurological soft sign abnormalities than in normal controls. In addition, some borderline patients manifest neuroendocrine abnormalities found in some patients with mood disorders, including short REM latencies and blunted prolactin response to fenfluramine, a serotonin agonist (Steiner et al., 1988; Cocarro et al., 1989). It has been suggested that central serotonergic function is reduced in patients with personality disorder and a subgroup of patients with mood disorder (Cocarro et al., 1989).

In a recent review examining the interface between borderline personality disorder and depression, Gunderson and Phillips (1991) conclude that the relationship between the two disorders is nonspecific. They favor the hypothesis that the two conditions "coexist but are otherwise unrelated" (p. 973). In a comparison of the pathogenesis of the two disorders, the authors state: "The evidence supports theories of heavy environmental loading in the causation of borderline personality disorder and, in contrast, of relatively heavier constitutional loading in the origin of usual depressive disorder" (p. 973).

But returning to the criteria for causation as defined by the epidemiologists, what do we actually know about factors that antedate borderline personality disorder? With the development of specific diagnostic criteria, there has been a dramatic increase in systematic investigations of the childhood experiences of adult and adolescent patients diagnosed as borderline. (For a review of the association between the family environment and borderline disorder, see the comprehensive review by Links and Munroe Blum [1990].) While impairment in the mother-child relationship was a focus of the early developmental model, more recent work has centered on the role of childhood trauma (Herman et al., 1989). In 1981, Stone speculated that one of the factors contributing to the greater number of females compared to males among groups of borderline patients was "the occurrence of incestuous experiences during childhood or adolescence" (p. 14). He pointed out that this issue had rarely been considered in previous studies of borderline disorders. The Freudian notion that most reports of incest were fantasies probably contributed to this omission, but perhaps none of us wanted to look too closely at the sexual abuse of children. Stone referred to a small sample of hospitalized borderline patients in which the incidence of incest was 75%.

During the early 1980s, a number of reports appeared describing an association between childhood abuse and adult psychiatric illness (Herman, 1981; Brooks, 1982; Carmen et al., 1984; Mills et al., 1984; Gelinas, 1983). Bryer et al. (1987) evaluated the rates of childhood sexual and physical abuse in a sample of 66 female psychiatric inpatients. A history of abuse at some time during their lives was reported by 72% of the subjects who completed the questionnaire. Fifty-nine percent of the sample experienced abuse before age 16. Within the group of patients who had experienced early sexual abuse, the most frequent axis II diagnosis was border-line personality disorder. Herman (1986) found a history of child-hood maltreatment among 67% of a small sample of patients diag-nosed as borderline.

This was followed by a study designed to evaluate the theory that borderline patients commonly have a past history of childhood trauma (Herman et al., 1989). Patients with borderline personality disorder were compared to patients with schizotypal personality disorder, antisocial personality disorder, and bipolar mood disor-der. A semistructured interview was conducted to obtain childhood histories. It is important to note that the childhood data were obtained by interviewers blind to the diagnoses of the subjects.

Eighty-one percent of patients with definite diagnoses of border-line personality disorder (five or more DSM-III criteria and a score greater than 150 on the Borderline Personality Scale) gave a history of childhood maltreatment. Seventy-one percent had experienced physical abuse, and 67% had been victims of sexual abuse. It is of note that patients diagnosed with borderline traits (at least four DSM-III criteria and a score greater than 130 on the Borderline Personality Scale) had a lower frequency of abuse histories, and that reports of childhood trauma were far fewer in patients with no diagnosis of borderline disorder.

The authors stress the strong association between a report of childhood trauma and a diagnosis of borderline personality during adulthood. It is notable that while the investigators highlight the importance of this association, they state clearly that no conclusions can be made about the causation of the borderline disorder because the associations are based on retrospective information about child-hood experiences.

But if indeed childhood trauma is of specific etiologic impor-tance in the pathogenesis of borderline personality disorder, fur-ther comparison with patients with other psychiatric disorders is necessary. As Terr (1991) has stated: "Childhood psychic trauma appears to be a crucial etiological factor in the development of a number of serious disorders both in childhood and in adulthood" (p. 10). In a study of male and female inpatients, Ogata and col-leagues (1990) compared patients diagnosed as having borderline disorder (according to the DIB) with control subjects without borderline disorder who met the Research Diagnostic Criteria for depressive disorder. There was a significantly higher rate of sexual abuse reported by borderline patients than by depressed subjects. Rates of physical abuse and physical neglect were not significantly different between the two groups.

In a study by Links et al. (1988), a group of inpatients who met the criteria for borderline disorder according to the DIB was compared to a group of patients with other personality disorders. Patients with a borderline disorder were more likely to have a history of childhood physical and sexual abuse than the comparison group. They were also significantly more likely to have been separated from their mother for a period greater than 3 months.

The three studies by Herman et al., Ogata et al., and Links et al. involved inpatient subjects. In a study of outpatients, Zanarini and colleagues (1989) compared the childhood histories of subjects meeting the criteria described in DSM-III (American Psychiatric Association, 1980), for one of borderline personality disorder, antisocial personality disorder, or dysthymic disorder. Subjects were assessed using the DIB, Diagnostic Interview for Personality Disorders (DIPD) and a draft of the Structured Clinical Interview for DSM III (SCID). These investigators conducted semistructured interviews blind to diagnosis to obtain information on childhood history. The authors chose two groups of patients (those with antisocial personality disorder and dysthymic disorder) who share specific symptoms of either impulsivity or chronic dysphoria, respectively, with borderline patients. While all three groups reported a high frequency of disturbed caretaking during childhood, a childhood history of abuse was reported by a significantly higher percentage of borderline subjects than patients with antisocial personality disorder or dysthymic disorder. Verbal abuse was reported by a significantly higher percentage of borderline patients than by those in the two control groups, while reports of physical abuse did not differentiate the three groups. Sexual abuse was reported by a significantly higher percentage of patients with borderline personality disorder than those with dysthymic disorder. Zanarini and colleagues (1989) also gathered information about the individual(s) who perpetrated the abuse. While the patients in the study of Ogata et al. (1990) reported a high prevalence of "non-parental abuse," involving siblings, cousins, uncles, and non-relatives, more than 75% of the borderline patients evaluated by Zanarini and associates reported a history of childhood abuse by their full-time caretakers. Within this group, approximately 50% described a history of physical maltreatment, 25% reported a history of sexual abuse, and approximately 75% reported a history of neglect.

Zanarini and associates (1989) explored the issue of separation experiences in the histories of these patients. The concept of separation included loss of the caretaker by death, marital separation, divorce, distant employment, hospitalization, incarceration, move or vacation or the subject's placement away from the caretaker. Seventy-four percent of the borderline subjects reported "one or more prolonged separations from a caretaker sometime before the age of 18" (p. 22). Notably, this figure was not significantly different from the percentage of patients with antisocial personality disorder and dysthymic disorder who experienced a prolonged separation before the age of 18. However, the timing of the separation experience(s) differentiated borderline subjects from dysthymic controls but not from subjects with antisocial personality disorder. The authors concluded that these results emphasize the role of abuse rather than separation experiences in the etiology of the borderline condition. This study, like others (Grinker et al., 1968; Gunderson et al., 1980), found that emotional neglect was common in the early histories of patients with borderline conditions. Zanarini and colleagues also stressed that a high percentage of borderline patients experienced more than one type of maltreatment. They suggested that for the development of borderline personalty disorder, "no one type of childhood experience is in itself sufficient" (p. 24). Similarly, in a recent review of the role of childhood sexual abuse in the etiology of borderline personality disorder, Paris and Zweig-Frank (1992) state "a simple association between abuse and the disorder is an oversimplification" (p. 125).

The study by Zanarini et al. (1989) was based on retrospective reports obtained from patients. Knoll (1991) has pointed out the potential for bias in such data. In a letter to the editor, he states: "The borderline patients of the present, much like the hysterical patients of Zetzel (1968) in the past, are well-known for distorting data and for initially trying to please the therapist" (p. 149). Knoll urges the validation of such data through additional "more neutral sources."

In 1980, Gunderson and colleagues carried out blind interviews with the families of patients with neurosis, schizophrenia, and borderline personality disorder. Within the families of borderline patients, there was a higher frequency of depression and psychosis among the mothers, and the parents were more involved with each other than with the child. The authors concluded that neglect was a discriminating characteristic among the families of borderline patients.

In 1981, Gunderson and Englund reviewed the existing literature regarding the families of patients with borderline personality disorder. They found that most reports of families had been based on material derived from clinical experiences without attention to systematic data collection. They highlighted the work of Grinker and associates (1968) as the best example of research that used a standardized evaluation. Nevertheless, Grinker did not use adequate control groups or explore specific hypotheses about the nature of the families of borderline patients. While Grinker discussed the issue of neglect, he also noted a characteristic of overinvolvement by parents. Despite problems with methodology, Gunderson and Englund (1981) noted the agreement among authors about the presence of "intense (dramatic) affective expressions within these families" (p. 167), regardless of the overall description of the family.

In their review, Soloff and Millward (1983) found no agreement among investigators about the specific interactions among family members that lead to the borderline condition. They then set out to explore the relative importance of three etiologic hypotheses in the developmental histories of borderline patients. These were (a) a neurobehavioral model; (b) a separation hypothesis, and (c) a family dynamic theory. The investigators compared the developmental histories of patients with borderline disorder (according to the DIB) with those of patients with depressive mood disorder and schizophrenia (according to Research Diagnostic Criteria). Unfortunately, the developmental histories were not obtained by individuals blind to the diagnoses of the subjects. Among the group of borderline patients, there was no increase in the incidence of neurodevelopmental abnormalities compared to that in both control groups. In evaluation of the separation hypothesis, Soloff and Millward (1983) did find an increased incidence of "broken families and parental loss (principally father)" among patients with borderline personality compared to control subjects (p. 585). In exploration of the family dynamic hypothesis, the investigators assessed five characteristics of the patient-parent relationship: positive bond, negative-conflictual, overinvolved, underinvolved, and consistent-stable relationship. Given the findings regarding the separation hypothesis, it is not surprising that the investigators found a pattern of parental conflict in the families of these patients. A negative-conflictual pattern was much more common among the families of borderline patients than among families of patients with depression or schizophrenia. Hostility and conflict characterized the marital relationship of the parents of borderline patients.

The study by Soloff and Millward (1983), like the childhood histories obtained from clinical samples, is limited by the problems associated with collection of retrospective information. The authors emphasize that "an ideal study would require a prospective survey of multiple family members, with interviewers blind to patient diagnoses, using reliable and valid assessment measures for each hypothesis" (p. 586).

In a more recent study, Zweig-Frank and Paris (1991) evaluated the role of emotional neglect and overprotection during childhood among adult patients with borderline personality disorder using a standardized measure known as the Parental Bonding Instrument. This is an instrument that measures impressions of parental behavior in the areas of care and protection during the first 16 years. While this information was based on the recall of patients, the data were collected using a self-report instrument with proven reliability and validity. The instrument was administered to a group of outpatients with borderline personality disorder according to the DIB and a control group of nonborderline subjects also drawn from the same outpatient mental health facilities. The borderline patients recalled less caring from their parents than did the nonborderline control group, but remembered their parents as more protective. The authors summarized the findings by stating: "Borderline patients are telling us that they remember their parents as both failing to provide basic emotional support and preventing them from separating" (p. 650).

Earlier work carried out by the same authors examining the recollections of family experience in borderline patients used a questionnaire called the Childhood Experience Scale (Frank & Paris, 1981). The recollections of the borderline patients were compared to the responses of a normal group of controls and a group of patients with neuroses and personality disorders. In this study, the investigators found that recollections about mothers among the three diagnostic groups did not differ significantly while fathers of borderlines were remembered as responding with less approval and greater disinterest than fathers in the other two groups. They concluded that excessive attention had been given to the mother and insufficient to the father in the etiology of borderline disorder. In a more recent study by the same authors, it is notable that recollections of patients point to failure in some aspects of caretaking by both parents (Paris & Frank, 1989).

The empirical work discussed thus far has focused on the histories of adult patients with borderline disorder. Certainly, many of the earlier theoretical developments arose from clinical practice involving adolescent patients (Masterson, 1971). Bradley (1979) evaluated a group of patients that included adolescents for a history of early maternal separation. Compared to a control population, there was an increased incidence of early separations among the borderline patients. Recently, Ludolph and colleagues (1990) compared a group of inpatient adolescent girls who met the criteria for borderline personality disorder according to the DIB with a group of nonborderline psychiatric comparison subjects. To obtain historical information, a chart review was carried out by a rater blind to diagnosis. The reliability of a sample of the data was checked by a second rater. The data collected included information about the life experiences and interpersonal relationships of the patients. Both groups had a similar rate of separation from parental caretakers during early childhood, including death of one or both parents. But there were significantly higher rates of adoption, sexual abuse, neglect, and protection-service involvement among the borderline adolescents than among the nonborderline psychiatric control subjects, and the higher rate of physical abuse came close to statistical significance (p= .06).

The authors concluded that no single traumatic event was associated with the borderline diagnosis at any specific period of development. And as Westen and colleagues (1990) said, in discussing causation of the borderline condition, problems in parent-child relationships coexist with experiences of maltreatment including abuse and neglect (Ludolph et al., 1990).

In a related study examining the incidence of maltreatment among adolescent patients with borderline personality disorder, this group of researchers raises the question of post-traumatic stress disorder and its association with borderline disorder (Westen et al., 1990). Famularo and colleagues (1991) evaluated a group of children and adolescents previously diagnosed as borderline personality disorder and found that just over one-third met the criteria for post-traumatic stress disorder.

Issues related to etiology clearly are not simple. Why do some patients with a history of childhood maltreatment manifest borderline symptoms during adulthood while others do not (Westen et al., 1990)? What is necessary and specific to the development of the borderline personality disorder? Retrospective accounts by adult patients fall short of providing us with this information.

We can say, however, that valuable data have been gathered on the association between reports of childhood experiences and borderline personality disorder, and progress has been made in the development of reliable and valid measures to diagnose the condition and collect data about these experiences. Rutter (1988), as cited by Robson (1991) in discussing borderline disorders in childhood, reminds us of the need to understand the "chain of operations" by which factors lead to disorder. Prospective studies would help.

It is clear that those people we call borderline in clinical settings tell us they have had difficult childhoods. Their difficulties include neglect, parental conflict, loss, and a disturbingly high incidence of physical and sexual abuse. This helps us understand them and their lives and even their current behaviors. But we can't yet say if any one of these things is etiologic. We also don't know what factors might prevent a neglected or abused child from developing a borderline personality disorder in adulthood. As Paris and Zweig-Frank commented in a recent review (1992), "It seems that any useful model for predicting the development of BPD [borderline personality disorder] must consider a combination of . . . factors and the way in which they interact" (p. 127).

Of course a childhood experience of neglect or physical or sexual abuse implies more than a traumatic experience. It implies a situation over time of very complex, confusing, and even paradoxical parent-child communications.

In later chapters the adult with borderline personality patterns is described as someone with unresolved self-system conflicts and ambiguities: good/bad, lovable/unlovable, kind/hateful, competent/not competent, in control/not in control. If this is a reasonable description and we wonder how someone like this could develop, extensive childhood experiences of neglect, abuse, and confusing, contradictory parental communication would fit the bill. Physical and sexual abuse must carry with them very troubling definitions of the child as bad and good, desirable and worthless, powerful and powerless, loved and hated—even bad and good and desirable and worthless at the same time. Furthermore, as mentioned in later chapters, these kinds of childhood experiences must impose an enduring sense of helplessness and incompetence.

But when one is confronted by a difficult borderline patient in a clinical setting, all these various ideas, theories, concepts, and empirical data usually don't provide a direct way of understanding and successfully managing the patient's most damaging and counterproductive current behavior.

This chapter and the work to which it refers are Cartesian in their organizing principles: They are predicated on linear causality, antecedents, and a chain of operations, and are developmental and reductionistic. Such explorations help us understand the substrate for the current behavior that we are trying to observe and document objectively. But managing and treating that behavior without doing harm, without contributing to disability, requires a small conceptual shift, a reframing.

The next chapter addresses that conceptual shift, and the one following attempts to integrate both paradigms before the specifics of treatment and management are discussed in later chapters.

# 3

# The Necessary Conceptual Leap

## Subatomic Physics and the Borderline Patient

At 11:30 one morning a therapist anxiously entered my office to tell me her patient, three doors down, was banging her head against the desk, sobbing, and loudly proclaiming that she was going to kill herself. Understanding that a prerequisite for crisis intervention is that at least one person not be in a state of crisis (Hansell, 1976), I had the therapist sit down and review the whole situation with me. When the therapist was reasonably calmed and I had a better understanding of the course of therapy over the past few weeks, I instructed her to go back to her office, tell the patient that they had done enough for today and that she would see her next week at the usual time.

The therapist came back to say that her patient had shouted at her that she was still going to kill herself and had rushed off in tears.

Not so certain of my judgment now, a little worried about what might happen to this patient, I gathered up my things and drove to the squash club for a lunch hour game. On my way through the lounge of the club, I looked to my left through the glass partition and saw, playing a vigorous game with much enthusiasm if not skill, the very person who had just spent a half hour banging her head against a desk, threatening suicide, and causing great concern to her therapist and her therapist's supervisor.

How should one understand this behavior? It might be said that in her therapist's office the patient dropped her defenses and displayed her true feelings and impulses. In the squash club she is demonstrating an ability to hold herself together when social circumstances dictate. But really she is very sick and very distressed. A second hypothesis is that this woman is indeed seriously depressed (has an affective disorder) but for short periods of time can suppress or overcome her illness.

A third hypothesis is that this patient is unconsciously displaying disturbed behavior in the presence of her therapist to achieve some goal unclear to the therapist and herself. A fourth is that this patient is manipulating her therapist, that she is consciously and willfully displaying disturbed behavior in the presence of her therapist to achieve some goal unclear to the therapist and the supervisor.

The first hypothesis suggests that the real person is very sick or disturbed but able at times to present a healthy but superficial front. Assumed reality in this case is an individual with a disturbance in psyche or brain.

The fourth hypothesis suggests that the real person here is healthy but for spurious reasons of her own presents at times with a very disturbed facade, which she could control if she wanted. The next step in this logic is that for the very reasons she finds it necessary to cover up health with illness, she must really be quite disturbed: Her healthy appearance is a facade upon which she constructs, on occasion, a further disturbed presentation. And onward, or at least upward and downward (because the metaphor here is depth) layer after layer. In fact the notion of depth permeates contemporary therapeutic practice. The surface is understood to be not real; underneath, in the core, are the real emotions and thoughts constituting the real person.

We are also usually certain that something has caused her disturbed behavior, something from her past, her recent past, or her present life situation. We may connect the past events and her present behavior in the office with notions of transference, but in our minds a sense of linear causality reigns supreme. When we ask why she behaved as she did, we answer ourselves with possible antecedent or precipitating events. We think of causation mainly as an event or series of events that can be understood to lead directly to the behavior we are observing.

Thus when observing and attempting to understand this woman's behavior, we tend to apply two fundamental organizing principles, depth and linearity, and two fundamental beliefs: that we can be objective observers and that what we observe is reality. This is because as Western therapists we are wedded to the world view of our culture.

In his *Discourse* of 1637, René Descartes expressed the ideas that primal self-evident data [can be] known with certainty, and no direct experience can ever deceive the understanding, if the understanding restricts itself precisely to that which is presented to it (1949). These have come to be known as Cartesian principles, and they have served science and medicine very well. They have allowed us to visit the moon, eliminate smallpox, control polio, and successfully diagnose and treat some affective disorders. They were revolutionary ideas in the 17th century but have become background in the 20th (ignoring for the moment New Age and *National Inquirer* influences).

We function and speak as if these principles were universal truths. Even when we speak of the unconscious and the Freudian concept of the mind, we assume that mechanistic principles are at work and that we can objectively observe the workings of another mind through its verbal productions, its dreams, and the behavior of the body in which it is located.

Isaac Newton first published his *Principia* in 1687, adding mathematical analysis to Cartesian logic. The modern science of physics was born. Natural phenomena could and would be understood by observing the behavior of component parts, formulating hypotheses, and using mathematics to deduce their consequences. The whole would be understood through an understanding of its parts (Hawking, 1988; Sen & Butler, 1989).

About 150 years later, John Snow played a significant role in propelling biology and medicine down the Cartesian pathway. A cholera epidemic raged in London. Two conflicting points of view were held equally strongly by opposing intellectual camps. The *miasmists*, pre-Cartesian in their thinking, believed that illness was somehow related to conditions in the atmosphere that affected the human spirit and body in a mysterious manner. The *reductionists* believed that diseases had specific causes that could be or would be eventually detected.

John Snow studied the pattern of this epidemic and wrote that the agent causing cholera behaved as if it were a living thing residing in water, though at the time no one had actually observed bacteria. He took out a map of London and noted the high incidence of cholera occurring in the population using a particular public water supply on Broad Street. The story told to generations of medical students is that Snow took the handle off the Broad Street pump, thereby reducing cholera in that district and ensuring the triumph of reductionist thinking in medicine.

But Descartes, Newton, and Snow did not attempt to observe and measure subatomic particles, nor did they attempt to observe, assess, describe, and treat the borderline personality disorder. It may seem a rather fantastic analogy, but the conceptual leap needed to come to grips with the borderline syndrome may be similar to that needed to come to grips with what is being called the "new physics."

At the subatomic level, physicists know that electrons sometimes display wavelike behavior, sometimes particlelike behavior—which one depends on the particular experiment performed. But, for reasons connected with the Heisenberg uncertainty principle, both wavelike and particlelike behaviors are never observed in the same experiment. Observed in one fashion, the electron is found to spin to the left. Observed in another fashion, it is found to spin to the right. The way they conceptualize the particle (wave) determines what they find. At certain levels of organization, we can predict only possibilities or ranges. The actual position of the particle or nature of the phenomenon (particle, wave) will be determined by the manner of our observations or measurements. Taking this one step further: The properties of subatomic particles may be creations of our own consciousness. What we see is determined by our conceptual models (Zukav, 1979).

In other words, uncertainty is present until we apply our consciousness and our tools, and when we then determine a certainty, it is in part defined by our own consciousness and our tools.

At the subatomic level of organization, the methods of Descartes and Newton have proved inadequate. Several scientist-philosophers have extrapolated from this discovery to a new way of viewing life, culture, the universe itself. This new viewpoint is difficult to articulate within the confines of logical, linear (Cartesian) Western thought and language. In fact, this new world view resembles an older, Eastern world view in which

> all may not be as it appears. Reality lies in the eye of the beholder. Mind and body are indivisible, as perhaps are human life, animal life, the planet, the very universe. If not indivisible, then at least inextricably bound. Nothing does or can exist in its own right. We must attend to relationships, not elusive and perhaps imaginary entities. The boundary between consciousness and objective reality is an illusion.

The Cartesian world view has made our thinking reductionistic and mechanistic and often prevents us from appreciating other realities: relationships, unseen connections, or as the physicists call them, "nonlocal forces."

When walking across the street, however, it is wise to apply a Cartesian frame of mind to the bus hurtling toward you. Undoubtedly the bus has substance; some*thing* is moving toward you at measurable speed with predictable outcome.

In medical circles and within the families of victims, there is usually no doubt that we should consider schizophrenia a disease entity, evidence of something wrong in the patient's brain. This way of viewing schizophrenia is leading us to understanding and effective treatment. This is not to discount the problem of the label being mistaken for the substance or referent, the tendency, once a schizophrenic is labeled, to view all the schizophrenic's behavior as originating in disease; nor is it to discount the influence of our institutions (mental hospitals) on our perceptions.

But when we conceptualize the borderline patient in the same manner, we find ourselves in trouble. Certainly it is possible to develop a consensus on groupings of traits and from this conclude that a syndrome is present. But in the process of doing this, we slip into a conceptual framework that also dictates our view of reality, our interventions, our treatment, the expected parameters of our relationship with the patient/client, the context within which we apply our interventions, and our interpretation of the client's (usually poor) response to treatment.

Like the physicists' electron, the people we call borderline may present to us possibilities and potentials, rather than substance and direction. Our presence, our observations, and our context will influence direction and definition. We meet them in a ready-made context (office, clinic, hospital, appointment with doctor or therapist, desk, diploma on the wall) that is already influencing their apparent substance and direction and our observations. We apply to them a conceptual model (analytic, dynamic, medical, object relational) with its own set of possibilities, and telegraph to them the parameters of this model. We meet them also within a tradition-bound social contract that implicitly defines interdependent roles, privileges, and responsibilities. For the sake of simplicity, we might refer to all of this as the *context* of our encounter with the borderline patient.

This context must to some extent influence the behavior of our patients and our observations of them. One would have to be an extremely self-contained, confident, stable, nonsuggestible, firmly bounded individual to withstand such influence.

The people we call borderline do not fit into this category (self-contained, stable). The context, of which we are a part, strongly influences their behavior. The social contract and our conceptual models strongly influence their behavior. Therefore our observations influence their behavior. The reality of the borderline patient merges with the context in which we participate, and we, as part of that context, have difficulty telling them apart.

This is not to suggest that borderline patients simply bend to the will of the therapeutic context or any other interpersonal context. But they are always responding to it with either compliance, opposition, or ambivalence.

Thus when we observe borderline patients and their presentation of self, we are really observing the product of the interplay between patient and context, or put more succinctly, the product of our own observations and expectations.

Not all is as it appears to be. . . . We must attend to relationships, not elusive and perhaps imaginary entities. The boundary between consciousness and reality is an illusion.

A major challenge in both the continuing exploration of borderline phenomena and the search for effective management is to find a way of utilizing both Cartesian and post-Cartesian organizing principles.

# 4

## Context and
## the Self-System

### THE INSTITUTIONAL CONTEXT

In any physician-patient encounter or developing relationship, there are at least two levels of communication. For shorthand purposes the first level may be referred to as the *content*.

> The 50-year-old man enters the office slowly, slumps in the chair, head bowed, eyes moving nervously. He speaks slowly. He tells the physician he has been feeling depressed for about 2 months, and off work and contemplating suicide for a week.

This patient has communicated to the physician, using language symbols as well as nonverbal and paralinguistic tools, information about himself and his experiences. The physician will assume that this information (e.g., feeling depressed, thinking about suicide, talking slowly, being unable to cope with work) represents an inner state, a psychobiological reality that is independent of the physician's office and presence. The physician will then attempt to understand this inner state and its implications using a logical diagnostic process and empathy. In fact, the physician will apply the two basic means by which we all attempt to understand the actions and feelings of another: empathy—that ability to imagine ourselves experiencing the life and feelings of the other—and a system of logical, linear causality. The limitations of empathy are worth noting. We are asking the question What *would it be like* to be him? (in which we place ourselves within the skin of the other, but bring our own histories and interpretive mechanisms) and not What *is it like* to be him? (which he can try to tell us but which we cannot arrive at through empathy).

The word "understand" could be replaced with the phrase "satisfyingly organize." In this example our physician is liable to use a disease model to organize the information presented, while a therapist of another stripe might utilize a psychological cause-effect model. Our physician will then form a hypothesis, ask questions to test the hypothesis, and come to a conclusion and recommend treatment.

Meanwhile, at the *process* level of communication, the patient and physician are negotiating a mutually acceptable role relationship containing a number of obligations and privileges. As Talcott Parsons (1951) put it, the sick role includes not being held responsible, exemption from normal social role responsibilities, being able to deviate legitimately, being expected to seek technically competent help, and to cooperate. Persons who are becoming patients may be requesting help, support, explanation, and exemption from certain activities and responsibilities, and requesting that the physician assume some responsibility for their welfare, their definition of self, and perhaps their safety. Our physician adopts a professional caring role if not in one already, and assumes some responsibility for the patient's well-being, self-definition (having a depression, being depressed, being ill), and possibly behavior. In return, the patient is expected to be honest and candid and to follow the physician's instructions and try to get better. This, in essence, is the development of a social contract. In this example the social contract has been prestruck, perhaps in part during previous encounters between the two participants, but primarily through social definition, tradition, and various codes of ethics and legislation governing the activities of at least one of the participants. Only the small print and other subtleties are left to be negotiated, or affirmed.

This social contract is tradition bound and context dependent (office, hospital, examining room) and establishes appropriate boundaries in the relationship (e.g., degree of intimacy,[1] responsibility, permanency, dependency). Unless either participant breaks the unspoken rules, or attempts to distort or alter the assigned and assumed roles, the social contract or role relationship need not be consciously examined. It serves most acutely ill people very well and, with some modification in the division of responsibilities, the chronically ill as well. (For pneumonia, the doctor prescribes antibiotics, the patient rests. For emphysema, a responsible patient would initiate, and stick with, a smoking cessation program.)

Though this role relationship or social contract is consciously examined in many forms of psychotherapy, the content level of communication usually remains paramount. This is the material brought to therapy. The therapist may observe, conceptualize, and comment on transference and countertransference events, but will still assume, and respond as if, the content of the patient's communication represents an inner reality independent of the therapist's presence.

Sullivan's (1940-1953) concept of "parataxic distortion" may help bridge the gap between transference and a more purely interpersonal level of analysis. This is a broader concept than transference and reflects his belief that it is "a notorious fact about personality problems that people act as if someone else were present when he is not, as the result of interpersonal configurations which are irrelevant to the other person's concern" (Sullivan, 1950, p. 330). Stolorow, Brandchaft, and Atwood (1987) move the concept of transference even farther along into the interpersonal field when they describe it as "a bipolar organization of experience, with continual oscillations in the figure-ground relationships between its selfobject and conflictual dimensions" (p. 105). Here they also are moving away from the notion of a patient's inner reality that can be known objectively, to a more context-dependent intersubjectivity.

Still, however transference is conceptualized, it should be noted here, if prematurely, that a transference interpretation is in itself content, a content-level communication. At a process level of com-

---

[1] This contract permits some very specific intimacies, while prohibiting others. It seems a strikingly high percentage of physicians transgress these rules with their patients, and so one might expect it would be even more difficult for therapists and physicians to adhere strictly to the fine print of their social contract with borderline patients.

munication, commenting on the possible meaning of the other's words or actions is a statement about relative expertise, relative competence, ascendency, and control over definitions of reality, or at least definitions of the current situation. These are the interpersonal parameters being negotiated, and as Jay Haley pointed out long ago in *The Power Tactics of Jesus Christ and Other Essays* (1969), the therapist is decidedly one up. A patient who is wont to dispute the ascendency of the therapist must undo the definition of the situation proposed by the professional.

The negotiation of a contract requires currency in its broad sense. The type of currency is determined by the nature of the contract, which is, in turn, context dependent. When the Godfather uttered the oft-quoted line "Make him an offer he can't refuse," he was referring to a kind of currency that would be used in the ensuing negotiation. If our patients wish to establish, enhance, or modify a medical or psychotherapeutic social contract, they will use appropriate or relevant currency. This currency will include verbal as well as nonverbal communication of symptoms, feelings, distress, and intentions, and will reflect the context within which the social contract is formed. The currency used will likely be a display of symptoms for a physician, internal distress for a psychotherapist, and social incompetence for a counselor.

This then is the institutional context of our encounters with those people we later call borderline: an established social contract and a situation that reinforces that social contract and dictates the currency through which further negotiations may take place.

## THE CULTURAL CONTEXT

There is a larger context at work that is well worth considering in this search for some satisfying organizing principles. This is the cultural context and, more specifically, the professional cultural context in which we describe the behavior of certain people, predominantly women, as borderline. A number of investigators have explored the fact that the preoccupation with an entity labeled borderline personality disorder is largely a North American phenomenon (Kroll et al., 1982; Macaskill & Macaskill, 1981, 1985;

Tarnopolsky & Berelowitz, 1984). It is quite reasonable to ask if it's possible that borderline personality disorders are so context dependent that they occur only in this particular culture, both general and professional; or, less drastically, if it's possible people are the same everywhere but that here, in distinction from other countries, a certain group of distressed individuals and our mental health professionals have come together to name, explain, and perhaps support some particularly disturbing behavioral patterns. Certainly it is generally accepted that schizophrenia occurs in all cultures, although the manner of its expression and the manner in which it is perceived are influenced by that culture. Possibly people with self-system organizations with the potential for that confluence of behaviors we call borderline personality disorder also exist in all cultures, but it is only our North American professional culture that supports this particular expression of distress.

We have always wished to understand, or at least to name (which carries with it an illusion of control), and yet be absolved of responsibility for, our discomforts, unhappiness, indecision, weakness, temper, distemper, inactions, and fatigue—even, in fact, to have them transformed into symbols of courage, martyrdom, and handicap. Historically, various branches of the medical profession have cooperated with this wish. The disease model nicely names things and sometimes explains them, and this naming enacts the social contract of the medical model that absolves patients of responsibility, and permits them to excuse themselves from certain expectations. Physical illnesses have always been more acceptable than mental illnesses. In the last century chronic appendicitis and then colitis were invoked to name and explain many vague discomforts. More recently, hypoglycemia was extremely common, and now we seem to be blaming just about everything on environmental hypersensitivity or chronic fatigue syndrome.

German physicians are prone to diagnosing patients who complain of fatigue as *Herzinsuffizienz,* or suffering from weak heart (Payer, 1990). French physicians are apt to blame a fragile liver for the same complaints. English medicine, within the polite, longer-view English culture, understands that it is not always better to do something than it is to do nothing. And American medicine can be aptly described as aggressive (Payer, 1990).

Is this pertinent? It is pertinent only in a cautionary sense. We live and work within our own cultures. We cannot view them objectively, and we cannot judge the extent to which the culture itself—its predominant values, forces, vectors, power mechanisms, and technologies—is influencing our perceptions. History tells us the influence is great, even on medical scientists. In the United States it became fashionable to see a psychiatrist and certainly more popular than in the rest of the world to view socially disruptive behavior, or what Goffman (1963) calls situational improprieties, as the product of complex psychological forces rather than simple motivated willfullness.

The authors are quite convinced that the worst of the behaviors of those people we call borderline are the product of our institutional and professional context. The main focus of this book is to convey an understanding of this phenomenon (the interaction of borderlines and the therapeutic system) and to explain and demonstrate a safe and effective way of changing these patterns.

Although there is a large preponderance of females in studies of borderline patients conducted in clinics (Widiger & Frances, 1989; Widiger & Weissman, 1991; Gilberston, 1992), different results might occur if other populations were studied (Ahktar et al., 1986). Males appear more likely to engage in a transactional relationship with legal and correctional authorities rather than medical and therapeutic authorities, and therefore are both defined differently and not absolved of responsibility for their (now defined as bad) behaviors.

## THE IMMEDIATE CONTEXT

Examples of communications from borderline patients are given in Table 1. These events usually take place in a context that assigns the recipient of the communication a number of traditional, professional, administrative, and even legal responsibilities that weigh heavily on and influence the recipient in an interpretation of them. When they are extricated from this context and presented as they are in the table, it is easier to see that the content of communication is servant to the process, to the immediate context.

## TABLE 1.
### Examples of Communications from Borderline Patients

Patient's sleeve slips up revealing several new cuts on the inside of her wrist.

*Therapist:* See you next Tuesday.
*Patient:* If I'm still alive.

Young female patient slouches in, glowering, sits in chair, keeps eyes on shoes, hair falls over face, doesn't talk.

At an outpatient team meeting you hear therapists discuss a patient you have never seen and use the following phrases:
"chronic depression"
"inadequate personality"
". . . kill herself eventually, sometimes there's just nothing you can do about it."

Patient weeps and weeps, nothing to live for, not able to do anything, can't make any decisions, doesn't know whether to come back or not.

Opening the session patient asks, "Did you hear that I was in emergency last night?"

*Patient:* Do you think I need antidepressants?

*Patient:* I'd like to stop the Valium, I can't depend on pills all my life.

Getting up from her chair at end of session patient accidentally tips her purse and a large bottle of aspirin clatters to the floor.

Supervisee bursts into your office and anxiously blurts that Mary, who she's been seeing for 2 years and who lost her job last week and had a fight with her boyfriend yesterday, is now banging her head against the desk and screaming she's going to kill herself.

Phone call at home: had to talk with you, really upset, just can't cope any longer.

Phone call at home slurred voice: can't go on any longer, won't be able to make appointment tomorrow.

Phone call at home: sobbing, tears, "Really sorry Dr. Jones."
"What's the trouble?"
Slurred voice: "Don't know."

Patient comes to appointment drunk.

*Patient:* "You get paid to see me. You don't really care what happens to me."

Bulimic patient tells you she has been doing a little better, only binged once last week, but feels fat all the same. You reassure her she does not look fat or even plump to an objective observer. After she leaves your office and you pick up a pen to make a positive note in the chart, you hear the distinct sound of retching coming from the outer washroom.

The content of communication from these borderline patients does not necessarily represent a persistent, consistent inner reality, but rather is dependent on the unfolding role relationship. It is the interactional process, the relationship the patient wishes to establish, maintain, test, alter, or distort that is guiding the content of communication, the patient's behavior, and essentially the creation of a social reality.

The immediate context of this role relationship would include the current state of the therapist (e.g., harried, confident, insecure, preoccupied, tired) and recent system events (e.g., conflict, suicide, lawsuits), all of which would of course influence the negotiations of therapist and client, and ultimately influence the definition of the situation at hand.

## THE SELF-SYSTEM

It is possible and may even be desirable to apply relationship management without attempting to conceptualize the psychic or self-system structure of the individual patient. Even if the independent intrapsychic structure of the patient is considered to be a black box, the interactional pattern of the relationship between this patient and therapist can be described and addressed. In fact, as mentioned earlier, when we stray from a purely interactional level of analysis to consideration of the patient's inner workings, we are often led, simply by the language we use, into first, a less than helpful perception, and second, counterproductive action (see case studies in Chapter 13).

Nonetheless, it is quite reasonable to ask why these particular people get in so much trouble within the contexts described above. The authors suggest that those people who find their way into the mental health system and are diagnosed as having borderline personality disorder are people with conflicted and/or ambiguous self-systems. As will become apparent later, the population and situations being addressed by this book are those in which the process level of communication is paramount, or those in which the here-and-now interpersonal negotiation is the more powerful determinant of the particular behavior being observed. If this is occurring between a client and a health care professional, it is reasonable to assume there is something about the self of the client that predisposes to this. (The exception, of course, is a very contained person with a good, unambiguous, unconflicted sense of self who forgets the reason for applying for patienthood, and instead is drawn into a vigorous interpersonal negotiation by a very disturbed, conflicted mental health professional.) For the most part, we can assume that there is a one-to-one relationship between those times when the process level of communication is paramount and some predisposing confluence in the self-system of the client. This one-to-one relationship may not hold, of course, for someone else's definition of borderline personality disorder.

The concept of self is both self-evident and the target of much convoluted theory. Fortunately, to achieve the goals of this practical book, we need touch on only the most pertinent theorizing. As most therapists know, when theories become very complex, they are of little immediate use in the practice of therapy.

George Herbert Mead, the symbolic interactionists, and Harry Stack Sullivan (1953, 1964) had much to say through the 1930s and 1940s about the self or self-system. Little of it, however, made its way into mainstream American psychiatry, which had clearly staked out two territories, the organic and the psychoanalytic. This also meant that through the postwar decades, the psychologically oriented psychiatrists and most other therapists were often deprived of the rich array of concepts and perceptions coming from social psychology and sociology. Not until some psychoanalysts themselves began writing about the self and interactional patterns did these become legitimate facets of theory and tools of therapy (Kohut, 1971; Kohut & Wolf, 1978).

Mead (1934) wrote, "Man's behavior is such in his social group that he is able to become an object to himself, a fact which constitutes him a more advanced product of evolutionary development than are the lower animals" (p. 137). According to Mead, "The self, as that which can be an object to itself, is essentially a social structure, and it arises in social experience," in "that process . . . of responding to one's self as another responds to it . . . being aware of what one is saying and using that awareness of what one is saying to determine what one is going to say thereafter"

(p. 140). Even if we now think that some of our primate cousins also are gifted with and suffer from at least basic self-awareness, there can be no doubt that the ability to be an object unto oneself is a central human burden. The trouble didn't start when Adam ate the apple; the trouble started when Adam observed himself eating the apple.

Heinz Kohut began the contemporary exploration of self-psychology by psychoanalysts. This in a broad sense is an attempt to go beyond and/or enrich mechanistic analytic theories. Kohut describes two components of the self, nuclear ambitions and guiding ideals. These, he feels, are derived from developmental transformation and internalization of mirroring and idealizing selfobject functions. Mead used the mirror analogy as well. Do they both mean that we act, and that then the other processes, responds to, transforms, and reflects back to us this information, which we then consume and store as symbolic representations of our selves? Kohut adds an idealizing process. As the information is reflected back to us, we may idealize it before storing it. Kohut further describes a flow of psychological activity between these two components or poles (nuclear ambitions and guiding ideals) as being the source of motivation. Stolorow and colleagues (1987) say that this concept is still too mechanistic, or thermodynamic (motivation arising by means of a tension arc between the two poles), and that it continues to confuse the self as both "an organization of experience" and "an initiator of action" (pp. 18, 19). They restrict the concept of self to the organization of experience and use the term "person" for the action initiator, and define the domain of empathic-introspective inquiry simply as the "organization of experience." The person, the action initiator, the motivator, the I, is beyond the scope of their brand of analysis. They are concerned not with their patients' motivation but rather with "whether or not they experience themselves as abiding centers of initiative" (p. 19). Stolorow and colleagues' intersubjectivity is certainly post-Cartesian; they emphasize the role of here-and-now context and subjectivity in the development of meaning. Still, the context to which they are referring is that of two people interacting, one of whom happens to be an analyst and one of whom happens to be a patient.

Attempts to pin down both the self observed and the observing self seem to lead down the same exhilarating slope followed by the physicists trying to pin down subatomic particles. Describing the observed self is one thing, trying to separate out the observing self is another, and leads to such brain teasers as Hofstadter and Dennett's *The Mind's I,* aptly subtitled *Fantasies and Reflections on Self and Soul* (1981). It is very natural to think of an "I" observing a self-system, and initating action, and of this I as the core, the real me, the soul. That may not be how it works. It may be simply that the self-system has self-referential properties, and that therefore this observing I is not a fundamental, irreducible, unsullied sacred core, but simply a property of the self-system, of the whole, of the full range of software running in our biological computers. But it may be worth noting, in line with the theme of this book, that the language and activities in traditional psychotherapies tend to reflect our belief that there is an I, a core, a soul within the behaviors and biology of the person sitting opposite us, and that this I is not a social construct. This is reflected in our questions about feelings, motivation, experience, and intent. Perhaps there is no homunculus within, but rather the I, the consciousness, may be a property of the totality.

Fortunately, for the purposes of this book, we can leave the problem of consciousness and the I, and the difficult journey from intra-psychic levels of organization to interpersonal levels, and focus in more heuristic terms on a way of thinking about the self-system.

The self-system must be formed through infancy, childhood, adolescence, and adulthood, but it must also be dependent on recent and present experience. The works of Goffman (1959, 1967) elucidate the power of immediate interpersonal and social experience on our sense of self and our presentation of self, and the extent to which our interpersonal behaviors are guided by the need to maintain, protect, or enhance our sense of self. It should be noted here that we don't really have to conjure up an I, an initiator, or central motivator to understand interpersonal behavior. Instead, we can think of the self-system as a system with built-in homeostatic mechanisms or organizing principles that, when impinged upon by external forces (other self-systems), operates first and foremost to *maintain* itself. Presumably, being socially derived in the first place, and given the universal phenomenon of entropy, the self-system must also seek encounters with other self-systems to maintain or refresh itself.

As briefly illustrated, the self-system can be conceptualized in a number of ways, but for our purposes can be described simply as embracing (a) fundamental attributes, (b) interpersonal attributes, (c) role attributes, and (d) supraordinate features (the manner in which the attributes are organized). Examples of these attributes or parameters within a self-system would be:

a.  Fundamental attributes
    good ......................................................... bad
    lovable ..................................................... not lovable
    strong ...................................................... weak
    competent .................................................. incompetent
b.  Interpersonal attributes
    responsible ................................................ not responsible
    loving ...................................................... hateful
    in control ................................................. not in control
c.  Role attributes
    healthy ..................................................... sick
    partner ..................................................... patient
    wife ........................................................ husband
    athlete ..................................................... scholar
d.  Supraordinate features
    stable ...................................................... unstable
    harmonious .................................................. conflicted
    clear ....................................................... ambiguous

These are listed as dichotomous positions because the resolution of the extremes of fundamental and interpersonal attributes is an important developmental task of childhood and adolescence (Mahler, 1971, 1972; Mahler & Kaplan, 1977). The authors suggest that those people we call borderline have arrived at late adolescence or adulthood without adequate resolution of some of these parameters. Healthy adults, by contrast, will carry with them a firm sense of being relatively competent, but vulnerable to a small temporary shift in the direction of incompetence that can be provoked by present experience. Present experience can shake their sense of competence, but they will bring healthy problem-solving mechanisms to the experience, learn from it, and return to a position of competence. A completely firm, unshakeable resolution of all parameters implies too rigid a personality.

Toward the other extreme are those people whose self-systems contain equal and conflicting attributes of goodness/badness, strength/weakness, competence/incompetence, and so forth.

```
< ------------------------------------------------------------------------->
   conflicted                              unconflicted
   unstable                                stable
   ambiguous                               clear

(very dependent on                  (less dependent on
here and now for                    here and now
self definition)                    for self definition)
```

One's self-system must have both historic and developmental roots and also be influenced by here-and-now experiences. Those who have developed, through childhood and adolescence, relatively unconflicted, stable, clearly boundaried, and organized self-systems will be less dependent on here-and-now experience for self-definition. Those with deeply conflicted and/or unstable and/or poorly boundaried self-systems will be inordinately dependent on here-and-now experience for self-definition. This latter group can be considered context bound. This is a major characteristic of those people we call borderline.

Borderline personality disorders must represent a spectrum, and in times of major stress or transition, when our self-systems are severely challenged, most of us display some borderline characteristics. For example, when stressed, challenged, and newly conflicted we all tend to externalize our conflicts into dialogue:

"I can't do it. They should get someone else."
"Of course you can do it."
"Christ no. I'm outa my league in there."
"You handled that meeting really well."
"Yeah? You really think so?"

"Except when Smith got out of control."

"Yeah. What can you do with a guy like that?"

"I don't know what to do. I just can't cope at work right now."

"It's understandable. You've suffered a great loss. Why don't you take a few weeks off?"

"But I'd go crazy if I didn't have work to come to every morning."

"Yeah, well, I can understand that."

"But I hate it. I don't have the patience."

A spectrum implies a range from severe to mild, from permanent to temporary. With reference to the degree of borderlineness of the structure of the self-system, this must be true. We can't all be alike. But with respect to the actual behaviors and psychiatric history of people with borderline personality disorder, the categorization of severe and mild can be misleading. With this disorder not all is as it appears to be. The behaviors are really the repertoire, the currency of choice or necessity, with which clients find they must negotiate interpersonal relationships. Multiple admissions and multiple mutilations may speak more about the collusion and needs of the institutions than about the severity of a patient's disorder. All is not as it appears to be.

She had been admitted to hospitals more than 80 times. Two community hospitals had prohibited her from further use of their facilities. Now, having been admitted to a third hospital following an insulin overdose, she smuggled an exacto knife into her room and proceeded to do to herself what the nurses described as a transverse laparotomy. This was severe. Or was it? When a management plan was organized and put into place according to all the principles described in this book, she behaved badly once more (tested the new contract), then left the hospital, lived in the community, took courses, attended day hospital, and has not behaved self-destructively nor been readmitted to date, a 3-year follow-up.

On the other hand, we run into patients whose troublesome behaviors amount to little more than noncompliance, missed appointments, failure to follow through, and yet seem to have a broader repertoire and a more tenacious need to re-create and maintain the borderline negotiations with health care professionals.

While the apparent severity or seriousness of the actual behaviors may be misleading, relative severity of the borderline state itself might be inferred by the relative generalization of the interactional pattern. If the client has no life situations, now or historically, in which the dominating distorted interactional pattern does not occur, it might be justifiable to consider the borderline state severe.

These characteristics or tendencies (the predominance of the interpersonal negotiation, the externalization of conflict) can also coexist with other disorders and illnesses, complicating standard treatment and compliance with treatment, and thus might be better labeled borderline phenomena, so long as we have to stay with the word borderline.

The management suggestions following in succeeding chapters can be applied to those that are perceived as severe as well as mild presentations of borderline phenomena, and to borderline phenomena coexisting with other illness and DSM-III-R Axis I diagnoses.

A state of conflict, instability, and ambiguity can be assumed to be uncomfortable. In contacts with (communication, relationship with) health care professionals and their institutions, the borderline patient is seeking resolution of self-system conflict and ambiguity, or, put simply, is seeking self-definition. As mentioned earlier, it would seem that female borderlines seek self-definition in their relationships with health and social agencies, male borderlines with law enforcement and correctional facilities. The majority of patients diagnosed borderline are female (Akhtar et al., 1986; Widiger & Frances, 1989), but the numbers of male and female borderlines would probably be more congruent if the diagnostic criteria were also applied to troubled young men who do *not* seek help with mental health agencies.

Unfortunately, they do not approach us saying, "I have this deeply conflicted sense of self, sometimes I feel bad, sometimes good, and wonder if you would help me." Rather, they present or display one side of the conflict, verbally, nonverbally, and behaviorally, utilizing content appropriate to the context. The content may be complex, dramatic, true or false, or partially true, and symptom and psychopathology laden, but is also and more importantly the vehicle or currency for the opening process proposition which is in the order of the patient being helpless/hopeless, not responsible, bad, sick, unlovable, or the like. This constitutes the externalization of the conflict and the transformation of it into dialogue. The therapist/physician will then convey in one fashion or another agreement or disagreement with the patient's proposition. The therapist may avoid responding at first, but will, inevitably, if only in subtle ways. If the therapist disagrees with the proposition—is in some way supportive, optimistic, encouraging—the conflict has then been externalized into dialogue. The patient may briefly accept the definition of self put forward by the therapist (it is not as bad as it seems, you are likable, you can cope, you can control yourself) but inevitably, and predictably, will reject it and/or be forced to display more vociferously the other side of the coin. The patient must attempt to prove or test the original proposition. The patient's conflict is then well externalized into a dialogue or nego- tiation, with the patient assuming the "bad" role and the therapist the "healthy, responsible, good" role.

An examination of hospital and outpatient records (and review- ing numerous cases with residents and other therapists) reveals that this typical interactional process leads to highly predictable and unfortunate results. The patient is forced to display and assume an increasingly bad position (incompetent, sick, helpless, not responsi- ble, suicidal) while the therapist and then the hospital assume greater goodness, control, competence, responsibility. Inevitably the therapist is forced to agree with the patient's proposition and consider hospitalization.

Once hospitalized, borderline patients will behave in one of three ways: They will accept, for now, the applied for and then imposed definition of self as sick, crazy, incompetent, and behave in an increasingly sick, irresponsible, dangerous fashion. Alternatively, they will reject this definition of self (the other side of the conflict being provoked into action—"I'm not that sick") and declare them- selves well and sign themselves out (possibly the best outcome of most hospitalizations). A third possibility is that they will declare themselves well, sign themselves out, and threaten self-destruction (vacillating between the good/bad, in control/not in control, competent/not competent definitions of self). This third outcome poses a great dilemma for the clinical team. These patients will probably be certified (imposing a legal/institutional definition of sickness and irresponsibility), and over the succeeding weeks their internal conflicts will be externalized and dialogued differentially with the staff (splitting). (While the technical analytic definition of splitting refers to the differentiation of internalized objects, we are using the word in its common clinical application: the observation that borderlines perceive some staff as good and some as bad, communicate to and about them accordingly, thus "splitting" them and causing or enhancing staff conflict.)

At some point they might be transferred from the community hospital to the psychiatric hospital, where, hopefully, they will reject the "very sick" definition of self and sign themselves out. Unfortunately, they may also receive vigorous biological treatment and all possible methods of external behavioral control. If we believe the origins of these disorders are related to childhood abuse, then clearly, at this stage of treatment, we have colluded with the patient to re-create and reenact childhood experiences. While professing and imposing a situational definition of care, concern, and responsibility, we abuse, shame, and assault.

When these patients are finally discharged, they will be referred to another therapist and the interactional process will begin again, with similar results.

We have suggested that borderline patients are seeking self-definition in their encounters with health care professionals. Of course they are doing more than that. As much as anyone else, they are driven to find both a resolution of internal conflict and ambiguity and a context in which their conflict can be maintained, expressed, and exercised. This can be seen as repetition compulsion. But there is a more satisfying way of viewing borderlines' interactional overdrive, the apparent determination with which they seek out and fashion the same interpersonal negotiation again and again. If the origins are abuse and neglect, then, as a child, the borderline was subjected, over and over again, to situations in which the adult imposed definitions of the situation contrary to the child's rudimentary perceptions. Thus while the adult is reflecting a confusing and conflicting array of attributes to the child's developing self-system (bad, good, lovable, hateful, desirable, shameful), the adult is also imposing a sense of helplessness and incompetence. The child has no control over the situation or the definition of the situation. The child is denied a shared way of understanding or mapping the situation, is denied the experience of a shared goal-directed interaction, and is denied the reciprocal validation of roles. The child must learn from this that the only way to overcome feelings of helplessness and incompetence is to control interpersonal situations with the tools and techniques available. Some effective ways of countering the situational definitions imposed by authoritative others are argument, passive resistance, demonstrations, street theater, recalcitrance, noncooperation, strikes, and self-harm.

So the patients seek self-definition, resolution of discomfort and conflicts, and engage others in the externalized dialogue of their central conflicts. Their presentation of self as helpless and incompetent stimulates the already controlling, definition-imposing, therapeutic authority, which makes them feel more helpless and incompetent, which they try to overcome by gaining control of the definition of the situation, using the currency at their disposal. This currency may include exaggerated displays of helplessness and incompetence.

Besides, there is a special kind of control over others that comes from not being in control of oneself. And there is a special kind of self-esteem and sense of power that must arise from being so chronically incompetent, hopeless, and helpless that one antagonizes and defeats the best and the brightest health care professionals.

And if this is the nature of the relationship sought by people with borderline self-systems, what more accommodating context could be found than our health care institutions?

# Part II

## Treatment of the Borderline Syndrome

# 5

## Principles of Relationship Management

The first three goals of relationship management are listed below. A summary of these principles first appeared in the *Canadian Journal of Psychiatry* (Dawson, 1988).

1. Do no harm.
2. Reduce chaos and curtail the distorted relationship between patient and health care institution.
3. Consider therapy.

Underlying the first two goals is the authors' conviction that the worst and most damaging behaviors of borderline patients are products of the unfortunate relationship between people with borderline personality organization and health care professionals. It is in the hospital that these people regress. It is in relationships with conventional therapists that these people act badly. This is not to deny the fact that borderlines regress and act badly in other relationships as well. It is simply that their worst and most dramatic behavior often occurs within their relationships with us, and that, unfortunately, we provide a context that embraces dangerous currency. As mentioned before, the accepted currency for interpersonal negotiations with health care institutions includes suicide threats and suicidal behavior, self-harm, mutilation, symptoms of illness, loss of control, conflict over medications, and helplessness. Besides, we are supposed to be helping.

Debate about this young woman's diagnosis had percolated for years. Did she have schizophrenia or did she have only a borderline personality disorder? In fact, at one time she had been referred to two research studies, one examining the psychosocial rehabilitation of schizophrenia, the other evaluating group treatment of borderlines. Each study used research criteria for diagnosis, yet she qualified for both studies. She dropped out of the one she entered.

What was clearly understood about her was that each of her hospitalizations had been difficult. She regressed, acted badly, on one occasion set her clothing on fire, and on another occasion was caught trying to set her clothing on fire, in the hospital. Now she was living in a boarding home.

One evening she argued with the landlady. She appeared somewhat irrational to the landlady, and she spoke of harming herself; in fact, she said she was hearing a voice telling her to harm herself. The landlady sent her to the general hospital emergency ward where she eventually saw the psychiatry resident. She told him her story, and then, while he was busy on the phone, she bolted and ran from the ward. He had the security guards bring her back, and he filled out the necessary committal papers.

He then called his supervisor, who happened to know of the case. He reported the patient's distraught condition, the fact that she wanted to go home, back to the boarding home, her suicidal ideation, her possibly psychotic symptoms, and the landlady's concern. During this time the patient unsuccessfully attempted a second elopement. The resident wanted her admitted involuntarily to the psychiatric hospital.

The supervisor explained to the concerned resident that this patient was known to not prosper in the hospital and that they should try to keep her out. He suggested a longer, slower approach with the patient, utilizing some of the techniques described in this book. The resident said he wasn't happy sending her home after she had spoken of suicide and he wasn't sure the landlady would take her back. The supervisor then outlined more carefully the relationship management stance and suggested that if the patient indicated at the end of the extended interview that she wanted to go home, that the resident simply first ask her to call her landlady and then let her go if she could talk the landlady into taking her back. The supervisor had used this latter idea many times before (having the patient call landlady or family member), and it had almost always stimulated a switch to competence. The supervisor went back to bed.

The resident did try this approach and the patient did become more rational and competent, but it was after one in the morning when they got to the part about phoning the landlady. The patient stated she definitely wanted to leave the emergency ward and go home, but she refused to call the landlady at this hour. The resident had made this a stipulation for returning home. Patient and resident argued. The patient remained adamant. It was now two in the morning. The resident sent her involuntarily to a bed in the psychiatric hospital.

It had been an interesting negotiation over control, power, and competence, and the result was possibly a draw. The patient ended the dialogue being competent, powerful, and controlling, while forcing the resident to treat her as incompetent and not in control. He in turn failed within a final display of power and control. That is the interesting part of this story. The tragic part is that this patient set herself on fire within a week of her admission to the psychiatric hospital and suffered extensive second-and third-degree burns.

In a later meeting with her mother, father, and stepfather, the mother verbalized the breakdown between empirical evidence and emotion that these patients provoke in all of us. It was pointed out several times to her, and she agreed, that on the three occasions her daughter had seriously and dangerously attempted to harm herself, she was *in the hospital*. Still, said the mother, when she's recovered in the burn unit, she must come back for a long stay in the psychiatric hospital because, obviously, she must be protected from herself.

The second goal, to reduce chaos and curtail the distorted relationship between patient and health care institution, may appear very modest. Traditional therapists may argue that this is simply good management, that nothing has been done to alter the deep psychic structures of the borderline patient. But there are two answers to this. The first is that helpful therapy cannot be conducted in an atmosphere of acting badly, acting out, chaos, regression, and repetitive distorting of interpersonal negotiations. (Although "acting out" has a technical definition referring to behavior motivated by unconscious conflict, in practice in clinics and on wards the term is apt to be applied to any bad behavior, however motivated. For our interpersonal perspective we will usually use the generic phrase "acting badly.") We believed initially that relationship management should be used to bring the therapeutic and/or institution-patient relationship under control and that then proper therapy could be applied. We have since come to believe that this "deep," uncovering, proper therapy is, for borderline patients, often detrimental, and sometimes serves our needs rather than the patient's needs. Thus the second answer: If the patient-therapist/ institution relationship is correctly managed over time, this in itself is corrective. It also provides a context *within which patients can help themselves.*

The third goal, to consider therapy, reflects our belief that it is not always better to do something rather than nothing. This is especially true when that something is to happen within a context that utilizes dangerous currency. Now it is quite clear in all human relationships that there are times when being helpful is not helpful. The trouble with borderline patients, of course, is that they insist on being helped, or people speaking for them insist they be helped (at times "helped" can be read as "controlled"), or they resist help but display behaviors that will inevitably bring help upon them.

In the beginnings of relationship management, one clinic devised three schemes for dealing with this problem, that is, for dealing with those patients who seemed to conduct troubling, harmful, dangerous, repetitive relationships with health care institutions. The first was a process of *"depsychiatrization."* This was an approach to shift the treatment of such a patient from the psychiatric clinic with its currency of illness, pills, suicidal behavior, and hospitalization, to a social agency with a less dangerous currency of social competence, employment, training, money, and so on. This could be achieved only through a close liaison between agency and clinic in which the patient's behavior was redefined as something within the purvue of the social agency. When this worked, it worked. These patients engage the workers in a social agency in the same kinds of dialogue with which they engage psychiatric services, that is, they negotiate the same interpersonal parameters, but the currency used is not as potentially harmful.

The second scheme was something referred to as "*no-therapy therapy.*" This was devised to answer the question, "How can we refrain from providing what we see as iatrogenic help (therapy, counseling) when the patients and their spokespersons are insisting we provide that help?" A straightforward refusal would bring about increasingly disruptive, dangerous, or threatening behavior, and we would eventually be forced to take the patients on.

So no-therapy therapy was invented. This was the offering of the form of therapy without the content. The form of therapy is a half-or full-hour (the time to be specified) meeting between client and therapist, once or twice a week, on a regular basis, in an office at the clinic. In this meeting both parties talk, the client more than the therapist, and both parties listen, the therapist more than the client. The therapist conducting no-therapy therapy would be instructed to offer such a regular meeting, perhaps declare that he or she wasn't sure of having any useful advice or suggestions to give, but could listen, and then, in the sessions, to do nothing. To do nothing meant not to help. Conversation was fine. Trivial conversation was fine. Sharing a coffee was fine. Giving information was fine. Being empathic was OK, if the empathic comment was devoid of inflection that implied anxiety, great concern, or responsibility. But asking penetrating questions, offering advice, guidance, interpretations, suggestions, or help of any kind were strictly forbidden. Not surprisingly, but it was surprising to some of the therapists asked to do this, some very troubling clients became troubling no longer, and, in fact, displayed a fair degree of competence. This was a rudimentary form of relationship management. Some of the distorted interpersonal negotiations were curtailed.

The third scheme was again born out of necessity. Some clients would come to intake with such checkered careers that no therapist would volunteer to "take them on," or "carry" them. These are the words of therapists and in themselves reflect the extent to which, even before seeing the client, the therapist is caught up in the distorted interpersonal negotiation. The therapist is already primed to "carry" the patient, as opposed to "talk with" or perhaps to "offer very specific services to" the patient. Indeed, with some of these especially troubling clients, a new therapist could get into difficulty before the first half hour had ended. In that short time the negotiations over control, competence, and responsibility may have led to feelings of fear and failure in the therapist.

The problem seemed to be that the therapists, in this case nurses, social workers, psychologists, and psychiatric residents working within a psychiatric clinic, would approach a first encounter with such a patient already assuming a stance of responsibility, control, and threatened competence. With these clients the therapists could imagine themselves donning the cloak of competence only to find it threadbare. Thus by assumed role, and a fear of failing in that role, they would be primed to engage in distorted negotiations with such a client.

So the problem lay in the assumed role and the therapist's need to be competent. How could we get therapists to meet such patients without the baggage of their assumed roles?

It is worth noting that these patients would come to us with multiple problems aside from bad behavior, and many past and current experiences with other would-be helpers and their instruments (programs, techniques, pills). And it was also worth noting that we didn't really know which of these problems was most troublesome to the client and what kind of interventions had actually ever helped.

Thus it seemed logical to ask these questions of such a client outside the distorted therapy relationship. Therapists assigned this task were told that in this task they were "not therapists, and must in fact declare this to the persons applying for clienthood upon their first and possibly only encounter. The therapist would explain to them instead that their job was not to help but to determine with the clients what specific kinds of help they might benefit from, *what they wanted*, in other words, from this clinic or other agencies. To aid a client in this task, and to distance themselves from the therapist role, they would spend much of their time on their feet at the whiteboard, noting, clarifying, specifying, and defining the client's problems and wishes as they were revealed. Clients, of course, would always be given ultimate control over these definitions of their problems and the proposed remedies. The *not therapist's* task was that of facilitator. It was also a rule that nothing could be left vague and abstract, in the way therapists love to talk about these things. So, for example, a client's "help for her ambivalent feelings toward her mother" would be refined as follows:

"What kind of help?"
"Someone to talk with."
"OK. How often?"
"Once a week."
"OK. How might the counselor help you with this?"
"Well, I'd like advice, but I guess they can't give me advice, so I suppose just listen."
"OK. You'd like a counselor to talk with once a week about your feelings toward your mother and the counselor only has to listen?"
"Yes."
"OK. What do you hope to get out of this help?"

These meetings, with even the most difficult clients, were surprisingly untroubled and free of distorted interpersonal negotiations. The result of such an intake meeting might be, for example, a very specific and realistic list of services being requested by the client, such as a 1-hour talk session with therapist X during which therapist X was expected only to listen and help the client clarify options, continuing to take pill Y prescribed by Dr. Z, dropping a relationship with agencies A and B, but having a meeting with the welfare worker, the therapist, and the low-rental housing agency to see if the client would be allowed back in.

Further evidence that the assumed and assigned roles of physician, therapist, and counselor are part of the problem lies within the observation that some research assistants specifically interviewing these clients to obtain data do not run into the same difficulties as therapists. The research assistant and therapists may in fact ask the same question, for example, "Do you often feel like killing yourself?" And the content of the answer may in fact be the same. But the contexts, the assigned and assumed roles and role expectations, put very different spins on the questions. When the client answers "Yes," and "Yes" again to the question, "Have you felt like killing yourself today?" the therapist cannot simply write down this reply and go on to the next question (as might the research assistant), and the client knows this. Thus the answers to therapist and research assistant may contain the same content, but will be given different inflections, and certainly will engender different responses.

A more elaborate statement of the third goal, to consider therapy, would be that, with borderline patients, we should always consider the possibility that doing nothing might be better than doing something, doing less might be better than doing more, and whatever is being done might be done in a safer context. Many of the techniques and principles explained throughout this book are more sophisticated elaborations of these early schemes of *depsychiatrization, no-therapy therapy,* and *not therapists.*

As a side note, it may be becoming clear to the reader that, for relationship management, theory did not precede practice. Rather, faced with the daunting task of helping and not further harming borderline patients, clinicians borrowed or devised a number of experimental approaches. Some of these proved dramatically effective, though they were quite at odds with established thinking and practice, and prompted the development of a model that in turn allowed the codification and further development of practice.

In keeping with the first three principles of relationship management is a fourth principle, namely: *avoid hospitalization.* A hospital ward is a loaded context, "loaded" in all its senses of full, complex, multiple, and powerful. Our client is context dependent. The transactional currency expands on a psychiatric ward to include seclusion rooms, one-to-one observation, physical and chemical restraints, control of "sharps," cheeked pills, hoarded pills, vomiting, heavier overdosing, deeper cutting, fire setting, suicide pacts, elopement, breaking windows, starting fights, interfering with other patients, hitting nurses, refusing to eat, refusing to get up, refusing to go to bed, provocative sexual behavior, . . . and more.

This loaded context presents an array of possible self-definitions, none of which is particularly positive, which the client can adopt or vigorously reject, independently, alternately, or contiguously. The context itself tends to define, label, and pin down the client, and alter the client's behavior and professed affective state. The negotiations begin the moment the client sets foot on the ward, and the possible currencies with which these negotiations will be transacted are quite awesome.

Beyond this, it is very difficult on a ward to alter the traditional social contract of the medical model. How can we explain to the director of nursing, the medical director, and the administrator our new contract with the patient that "should you cut yourself or harm yourself in any way we will fix you up medically but nothing else will change—no restrictions, no closer observation, no security"? And further, how can we handle our anxieties about explaining this new social contract to the hospital lawyer if something goes wrong? Within the traditional social contract of the medical model are oft-repeated significant phrases used after something does go wrong: "We did everything we could." "She received the best of care." The fact that "everything we could" may have hastened death or increased discomfort seems less important than the stated fulfillment of the medical contract.

The multiple personnel of a hospital ward offer fertile ground for engaging in a differential dialogue, or splitting. It is almost impossible to stop. No matter how closely knit the team, how clear the treatment plan, how convincing the leader, somewhere on the ward there will be a staff member who believes we are being unfair and unsympathetic to the poor patient, and another who believes we're all being manipulated. (The word "manipulation," though commonly invoked on wards and in clinics, and though having a useful technical definition, is often used pejoratively to imply the behavior at hand is consciously and maliciously motivated. Bad behavior from a bad person. We stay away from the word and instead use such terms as interpersonal negotiation, currency, gambit, ploy, test of social contract, and part of a repertoire of negotiating currencies.)

A fair number of papers (Adler, 1973; Friedman, 1969; Wishnie, 1975; Drum & Lavigne, 1987; Gabbard, 1989b; Main, 1957; Silver et al., 1983; Silver, 1985) describe the problems of regression and splitting in inpatient treatment. Some, however, have been written by psychiatrists still convinced of the charms of intensive psychotherapy within a holding environment, of regression in service of the ego, and end simply with a cautionary note. The distressing aspect of some of these papers is twofold: Elegant theory appears to overwhelm contrary empirical evidence, and the negative social and self-percept consequences of any psychiatric hospitalization are ignored. This latter consequence, as any articulate ex-psychiatric patient, will tell us, or "psychiatric survivor" as they now tellingly call themselves, is profound. Increasing concern about lengthy admissions is being expressed in the literature, but it is difficult to know what is actually happening in practice.

One paper with a lengthy case history describes a graduate student of English literature coming to the counseling service of the university for some help around exam anxiety and relationships. She appears relatively competent in her external affairs but is diagnosed as having borderline personality disorder. She is engaged in uncovering, interpretive, psychoanalytic psychotherapy. The author reports, quite blandly, that in one session she regressed, had a rage reaction, and was hospitalized. The case report is illustrating something else and does not dwell on the hospitalization.

This is reminiscent of the older literature on the inpatient intensive psychotherapy of schizophrenia. More than one paper illustrated the value and success of some psychoanalytic techniques with lengthy case studies that ended blandly with something like, "Unfortunately, after 9 months of twice-weekly meetings, with the patient just beginning to show signs of improved ego integration, he hit an attendant and had to be transferred to the state hospital." The elegance of the analytic formulations and the therapist's subjective impression of improvement are seen as more significant than the fact and consequences of the violence, the possible causes of the violence, and ways of preventing and managing such violence.

There can be little doubt that some regression, in the sense of one's feeling and acting like an "orphan" (Pearson, 1989), may be a natural and necessary component of the journey of change. We all benefit from occasional lapses into childlike behavior. And people who do not have borderline personalities may profit greatly from occasional episodes of psychological regression within a supportive, trusted relationship. However, psychiatry's history of regression as treatment, or planned and provoked regression, is, to say the least, spotty. It seems when we take charge and promote such regression the result is as likely to be harmful as it is beneficial. Besides, power corrupts, and the counterpoint to establishing an environment and relationship designed to promote regression is the assumption of a powerful, all-wise, paternalistic position. Couple this with an elegant theory, some ambition, and we are on dangerous ground indeed. The embarrassing revelations about Ewen Cameron's work at the prestigious Allen Institute are indeed cautionary (Gillmor, 1987). Of course, it is the bias of this book that with borderline clients we should be doing things that promote competence right away, and not after a journey through regression, despair, acting badly, and self-harm. Thus, *do not hospitalize*. (Later chapters will address the techniques used to safely prevent hospitalization, and describe ways to make hospitalization as trouble free and productive as possible when some borderline clients inevitably find their way to the inpatient service.)

In keeping with the principle of reducing loaded contexts is the advice to have *same-sex therapists*, especially for any therapy of length. The exception to this advice would be for homosexual clients or homosexual therapists. This is contrary to the assumptions held in psychoanalytic therapy, in which it is suggested the sex of the therapist doesn't matter. Transference and countertransference are not confined to gender. But there is no doubt that male therapists have a harder time not responding to distressed young women as potential protectors, fathers, and lovers; and female therapists may have trouble not being intimidated, angered, or excited by the sexually swaggering young man, or responding as mothers to sad boys or as disappointed wives and daughters to inadequate, dependent male clients. We already know the borderline patient is having trouble with projections and distortions. Why make things more difficult? Especially when the rule of therapy with borderline patients is *not* to engender a transference or parataxic distortion so that it can be interpreted, but rather to avoid as much distortion as possible.

Some years ago the male resident treating a young woman brought his audiotape to the supervision group. The content of their discussion on tape seemed quite reasonable, and the group set about offering formulations and interpretations, asking why he hadn't picked up on comment Y, or why he had asked about subject X. The supervisor tuned out the content and listened to the music of the therapy, the tone, tenor, modulation, prosody. He then asked the group to do the same. He asked the group where they might have heard similar music, similar tone, and pacing. He answered his own question. In the bedroom. It was bedroom talk—those particular tones of secrecy, intimacy, and subdued excitement usually confined to the bedroom.

How do we keep this relationship from implying more than it should? Conventional wisdom suggests you bring the subject up and talk about it. She says she is attracted to you. You say you find her attractive, too, but then go on to explain the bounds of therapy, the boundaries of this professional relationship, and the fact that this relates to transference and countertransference. It is safe to have these feelings because they will not be acted upon. Of course, recent disclosures indicate it has not been safe to have these feelings with approximately 10 percent of therapists (Gartrell et al., 1986).

But to avoid the unethical—and now in some states and provinces, criminal—behavior of acting on these feelings in a therapy relationship, how can the feelings be discussed and put aside in other than a titillating manner? It's something like the married man saying to his lunch date over coffee after a warm, intimate luncheon, "I think you're very attractive, but I don't want to have an affair." And then she says much the same to him, and they both feel better having said what they said, and they know they really shouldn't, but they'll have lunch again pretty soon, and maybe their ritual incantation will protect them and maybe it won't, and it's really all quite exciting.

Well, maybe it can be handled with most clients (Edelwich & Brodsky, 1991). But borderlines *arrive* with distortions, projections, and wrong-headed expectations. Why make it more difficult for them and ourselves? Furthermore, there is a good chance the female borderline will want to talk about, and may benefit from talking about, her experiences of sexual abuse. Isn't she more apt to do this with a woman?

Every year in a small residency program it comes to light that a male therapist is going for walks along the trails with his female borderline client. Breaking the set of therapy, changing the context, can be a good ploy, especially with apparently depressed, sulking, passively angry teenagers. The atmosphere and the client's responses may change dramatically when therapist and client walk side by side, sit side by side on a park bench, have coffee at a lunch counter, shoot pool together. Same-sex therapists can do this. Opposite-sex therapists cannot do this without sending a nonverbal message that is better not sent.

We do respond to apparently vulnerable, fragile, young women differently than we do men—male therapists especially do so. Female therapists are more likely to notice the power within the fragility and vulnerability of the small young woman. It is also less likely to be exercised on a woman therapist. Better to give this client to a woman therapist who does not view her client through the culturally determined, and maybe even biologically determined, filters of the male protector. It is an interesting exercise in supervision to ask the therapist or team struggling with the helplessness, threats, and self-mutilation of a pretty young woman to imagine her as a same-age male, perhaps 6 feet, 200 pounds, tattoos on his upper arms, bearded, booted, denim-jacketed, his Harley parked outside, but saying and doing the same things. What are their feelings now, be they countertransference or not? Do they still wish to protect the person? Do we now see the person as responsible or not responsible?

## Meaning Found in the Moment

She is overweight, childlike, but clever, and very adept at gathering would-be rescuers around her. After 27 admissions, she has garnered many of the labels available in DSM-III-R. On her fifth admission, she acquired command hallucinations and became, as recorded in the opening note of several succeeding admissions, a "well-known schizophrenic." Now when she leaves her therapist's office in a huff, climbs to a prominent but inaccessible place, and cuts her legs with razor blades, she tells us the voices told her to do it.

When I'm brought in to see her for the first time, she's sitting up in an infirmary bed with her newly bandaged legs. Before I'm introduced to her, she plaintively asks, "Do you think I'm hopeless, Doctor?"

By culture and training we tend to seek meaning in linear causality and antecedent events. So we might ask, "Why do you think you might be hopeless?" or "What's been happening to make you feel this way?" or, "What upset you so much in the therapist's office?" or, "Tell me about the voices." But with the patient in the above vignette the more important meaning resides in the fact of the consultant's entering her room, her lying bandaged in an infirmary bed, each of them in their respective roles and her asking this of him now, opening with this particular question, in this particular manner. To grasp this meaning of the moment we must look to the process level of communication.

## Process Level of Communicaton as Paramount

It would stretch the credibility of any therapist to claim this question, "Do you think I'm hopeless, Doctor?" could be read as straightforward content, or simple text, but to make the point, consider it as such for a moment. It is a question asked by one person of another, regarding the second person's opinion of the first person. It calls, logically for one of several answers, including, "No," "Yes," or "I don't know." Of course the second person has the option of being honest or not.

At a process level this patient is presenting herself as helpless, and she asks the consultant to decree her state of competence (hopelessness), to define the situation. In his role as physician, he is expected to be at least encouraging. The opening lines of this dialogue are already scripted. This is the first line of an interpersonal negotiation. From the one line it is difficult to know exactly what interpersonal parameters will be negotiated, but the context and role expectations can help us guess this. The consultant, if he follows the script dictated by his role relationship, must in some way convey to her that he doesn't feel she is hopeless. We know what will probably ensue is the client's then proceeding to explain or demonstrate why it is she should be considered hopeless. Thus the client is hopeless (incompetent), the consultant is wrong in his opinion, and therefore also incompetent. She has redefined the situation. The consultant will undoubtedly try to regain his position of competence, and the negotiations will continue. It is this level of communication that will impact on her self-system and her behavior.

## A Social Reality Being Created

What is the reality of this person? Is it immense disability implied by 27 admissions? Is it this childlike and helpless presentation? Is this someone with no control of her own behavior as implied by her self-mutilation and by the many diagnoses we apply to her?

The consultant's perceptions are being shaped by information, and his role position predisposes him to accept certain interpretations. If he steps out of his role, however, he might notice the immense skill, sophistication, and self-control also implied by this interpersonal behavior. Which is real? Is she childlike and helpless or is she powerful and controlling? The patient and consultant, in dialogue, will be negotiating that very question. That is, through the negotiations of the parameters of their relationship they will be defining her social reality.

There are no absolutes here. Personality disorder is a concept. Dependency is a concept. Inadequacy is a concept. The reality will arise out of the social encounter.

## All Not as It Appears to Be

The consultant entered the team meeting as they were discussing a client who was on her way into the clinic to see a therapist. This was a special appointment set up because the therapist was worried. The client had been admitted twice to the hospital recently, and now throughout her sessions with the therapist continued to weep and talk of her hopelessness, indecision, and suicidal thinking. The therapist was also feeling hopeless, and the team

leader was talking about the woman's dependency and inadequacy, and how maybe she couldn't be helped and would probably require further admissions and might eventually kill herself. (She dressed well, attended to hygiene and makeup, had
no sleep or appetite disturbance, and was not considered to have
a primary mood disorder.) When the consultant heard the words
"dependency and inadequacy" and the prediction of disability
and suicide, a bell rang in his head. He joined the group and
told them all may not be as it appears to be, and instructed the
therapist in some of the techniques in this book. The therapist
then saw this client with the consultant and team watching
behind a one-way screen. Despite the instructions, the therapist
was in trouble very quickly. The patient was weepy and hopeless,
unable to make any decisions at all, and the therapist was advis-
ing, suggesting, encouraging, and becoming increasingly frustrated. The consultant took over the interview. The question that
immediately arose was whether or not the client should continue
seeing the therapist. At face value it was a relatively unimportant
question considering the larger issues of hopelessness and suicide. But the consultant knew that the content of the question
was unimportant, that it still reflected the fundamental parameters being negotiated. Therefore the consultant stayed with that
question. For the next three-quarters of an hour the client,
through weeping and protestations of hopelessness, tried in
dozens of different ways to get the consultant to advise her on
continuing or not continuing to see the therapist. For the same
three-quarters of an hour, deftly, and sometimes not so deftly,
he sidestepped the question and gave it back to the client. In the
end *the client decided* to return to see the therapist. Next week's
appointment was established and the session terminated. Over
the next few sessions, the client (with the therapist now using
the relationship management approach) stopped weeping,
made several decisions about her life, and then terminated therapy after a couple of months. Last seen, she was competently
shopping in the local grocery.

Underlying this apparent chronic dependency and inadequacy was an interpersonal negotiation about competence and
responsibility.

Another patient was quite notorious locally and considered very difficult, angry, and dangerous by therapists in several clinics. Yet in the role of advocate and spokesperson she sat in the medical director's office and with great thought, clear perceptions, impressive insight, and fairness, discussed for half an hour problems that existed in patient care on one ward and ways they might be improved.

All is not as it appears to be. In the "Do you think I'm hopeless, Doctor?" vignette, the patient's history, her story, her statements, and her presentation will all lead us to some conclusions about her reality. These are socially created realities. There is equal potential for other realities, or other interpretations of her story. When we come across someone labeled passive, dependent, or inadequate, it is salutory to take a step back and make note of the battleground littered with the bodies of dozens of would-be professional helpers. Then ask again. Who is really powerless and inadequate in this situation?

## Statements and Gestures as Propositions

The words "Do you think I'm hopeless?" or "I can't cope" or "I'm hopeless," coupled with synchronous situation, posture, cadence, prosody, and facial expression, should be understood as interpersonal gambits or propositions, and not necessarily representations of a consistent, persistent inner reality. It should be noted here that the words may represent an internal feeling state or an interpersonal ploy or, at times, both.

## Content as Servant to Process

Why did she ask, "Do you think I'm hopeless?" when the consultant entered the room? She's in an infirmary bed. He's the medical director brought in to consult on a case obviously frustrating the therapist. They are about to define and negotiate their relationship. The question fits the context and should engender either an encouraging "I don't think so" or "Nobody's hopeless" (in which case she can then *tell* him how wrong he is), or a series of questions designed to lead her to a hopeful conclusion (in which case she can *show* him how wrong he is).

## Context-Bound Presentation

She is context bound or field dependent. We should not be surprised to find her depressed and helpless in the infirmary bed, then arguing with her mother on the phone, then happily talking with visitors. One presentation of self is no more true than another.

## Drive To Re-create a Pathological Relationship

Now unfortunately, she is not merely seeking self-definition. If this were true, we could help her with the application of positive regard and self-esteem building activities. Rather, she is driven to create or maintain or re-create a particular type of relationship, within which a particular interactional pattern will be endlessly repeated. The parameters of this relationship will be those of all relationships: power, control, ascendancy, competence, responsibility, intimacy, dependency, permanence. But she will be attempting to develop a relationship in which she can express, in sometimes alternating and sometimes contiguous fashion, both sides of her divided or conflicted sense of self, and have them reflected back to her in a repetitious and predictable fashion. (See the previous chapter for a more extensive discussion of this interpersonal dynamic.) The script is already written. We can't directly change her part. We can choose to change our part.

How do we do this?

## ANALYSIS

1.  Apply an interpersonal (or dramaturgical) analysis to (a) the pattern of her relationship with health care professionals and institutions, (b) a single encounter.

Different language is needed to shift from our usual medical/ disease or psychodynamic models to an interpersonal model. When we think and talk about a client, our language betrays hidden assumptions of linear causality, cause-effect relationships, internal psychobiological mechanisms, and motivation.

> Following a fight with her boyfriend, she felt very depressed, decided she wanted to die, and took an overdose.
>
> A dramaturgical way of telling the same story would be: She argued with her boyfriend. One-half hour after he left, she swallowed a small quantity of pills. She then called his apartment. She spoke to him. He came back and brought her to the hospital. Her stomach was lavaged. When I entered the room to interview her, she was sitting sullenly in a chair, hair hanging over her face. She asked for a cigarette. When told I didn't have one, she asked in an angry fashion if she could leave. When asked why she took the overdose, she said, "Why do you think?" When asked if she had wanted to kill herself, she said, "Of course. Now can I go?"

The interpersonal analysis will sidestep motivation, illness, and internal states, and focus solely on the relationship parameters being negotiated first between the client and her boyfriend and then between the client and the interviewer. (Several brief case histories are presented in traditional format in Chapter 13 and then translated into an interpersonal level of analysis, although it will be noted that important information is often missing in traditional formats.)

The same interpersonal parameters are being negotiated in the single encounter and the lengthy relationship with the health care institution. The microcosm and macrocosm follow the same organizing principles. In any given case it may be easier to see the patterns clearly in one or the other.

2. From this develops an understanding of the relationship parameters being continuously and constantly negotiated.
3. Understand these parameters as dichotomous positions.
4. Understand the negotiations as two- or three-act plays.

If the interpersonal negotiation is about competence/worth, the extended (natural) transaction will follow one of a limited number of patterns:

a.  Client presents as hopeless (incompetent). Therapist engenders hope (competence). Client accepts this, leaves interview saying they feel better.

   However, at next encounter (telephone that night, emergency room that night, the day before next appointment, or next appointment), client reports feeling more hopeless (more incompetent). Therapist engenders hope. Client accepts this, leaves interview feeling better.

   Pattern repeats.

b.  Pattern a is played out in single interview.

c.  Display of incompetence on part of client increases, and display of competence on part of therapist increases with each new encounter (ideas, suggestions, programs, pills).

   Therapist engenders hope but offers to see client more often, thus giving double message: You are competent, but I'm worried about you. Client utilizes more dramatic currency.

5.  Understand the predictable and natural outcome of these negotiations if they proceed unchanged.

This dialogue is the externalization of the client's internal conflict. In the first act the client displays incompetence; the therapist assumes the competent position. This is tested, developed, perhaps with several variations, in the second act. Eventually, however, the client's continued incompetence threatens the therapist's position of competence. Now to remain competent, the therapist may have to admit or agree with the client's position of incompetence, and, for example, arrange hospitalization. Now that the therapist is at least partially accepting the client's incompetence, and at least partially failing, the client will move in one of three ways: The client will now switch to competent (sign out of hospital), proving the therapist's incompetence, or continue the same dialogue with more dramatic currency (see above), or oscillate between competence and incompetence (sign out, claim to be still suicidal).

In the predictable third act the incompetent or oscillating client has forced the therapist into a position of failure (incompetence), and the therapist will then reject the client (transfer the case, refuse to do follow-up, fire the client, or something similar).

With an understanding of the process-level communication and the interpersonal negotiations taking place, the patterns described above can be quickly and dramatically changed through the following stance and techniques, of which many examples will be offered in later chapters:

1. Avoid your assigned role position.
2. Immediately correct when you discover you have assumed a distorted role position (father, mother, rescuer, teacher).
3. Assume a warm but benign, neutral posture.
4. When necessary, assume a posture that is contrary to the one assigned or expected.
5. Use paradoxical interventions when necessary.
6. Overtly present and discuss the new social contract.
7. Always assume the client is a responsible, competent adult.
8. But overtly set absolute limits or boundaries according to your or your agency's or ward's resources and tolerance.
9. Set consequences you are prepared to deliver.
10. Be carefully honest.
11. Apply these principles to all issues (medication, mutilation, suicide, programs, drug/alcohol abuse, length of stay, and so on).
12. Bring family members and other helpers, agencies, and third parties into this plan, if possible; otherwise, apply the same management principles to them. Control that which can be controlled; do not attempt to control that which cannot. When necessary, view family members as part of a borderline system, and dialogue with them as if they constitute one organism.

## Prerequisites for Applying This Model

1. A belief that the client is at least potentially competent and responsible.
2. Internal work by the therapist (e.g., must like patient, know own personal vulnerabilities). Must not use this approach as a covert way of getting rid of the patient. The major danger with relationship management is that it can appear to give some staff and therapists license to express feelings toward the patient that have up to now been buried, denied, exorcised through reaction formation, or simply suppressed by the traditional display of a professionally empathic attitude—as Main (1957) put it, there is a "temptation to conceal from ourselves and our patients increasing hatred behind frantic goodness"(p. 130).
3. Assessment of the institutional context (tolerance, anxieties, recent suicides, conflict).
4. Supervision or consultation. It is extremely difficult to use relationship management without at least peer supervision. The therapist is being asked to think and perceive quite differently and to ignore many of the things to which he or she has been trained to hear and respond. At a superficial level relationship management seems to deny the expression of those very qualities that probably guided the therapist's vocational choice: empathy, concern, helping, and caring. Of course, our claim is that the unsophisticated and unbridled display of these qualities harms borderline patients and that using the apparently less empathic relationship management approach ultimately provides better care and help.
5. Team and ward staff must agree with approach to prevent conflict, mixed messages to the client, and dialoguing differentially (splitting).

## Special Problems

*High Lethality.* There are some borderline patients who engage in particularly damaging or potentially lethal activities, usually in the context of continuing traditional management with repeated admissions. Consideration of potential lethality is not to be mistaken for our usual self-destructive behavior categorizations of serious or not serious, which are an inference of intent. We cannot know the intent, but we can understand the relative potential lethality of different events (e.g., six diazepam vs. insulin overdose). Potential lethality and our anxiety about potential lethality may make it difficult to set one of the recommended limits and consequences (immediate discharge, never admit to hospital), but a modification will achieve the same goal, which is to exclude self-destructive behavior as legitimate currency in these new interpersonal negotiations: "Should you cut yourself badly, we will attend to your injury and fix you up medically, if you allow us to, but nothing else will change. You will not be made involuntary, secluded, restrained, or more closely watched, and you can still leave any time you decide to."

## Central Dialogue with Someone Else

It was known that the patient had been seeing an external therapist three times a week. The therapist declined to attend a case conference after his client was admitted. In the evening the ward staff overheard the patient talking on the phone with her therapist and saying, "If you don't come and see me, I'll kill myself."

The problem doesn't reside in whether or not the therapist will come in but in the fact that the patient is involved in a major dialogue or negotiation with an external professional. On this stage the staff of the hospital are merely spectators, bit players, and conduits. This is always a dangerous and untenable situation. The outpatient therapist must attend and participate in the case conference, or terminate. If the outpatient therapist refuses, then immediate discharge to his or her care should be considered.

*High Profile.* Some patients are well known to nursing office, police, community agencies, and so on, all of whom wish the treatment team would contain and control the patient. To whatever extent possible, these people should be brought into the management plan. One way of achieving this is with a large case conference, all helpers attending, the patient attending, and the patient placed in control of the meeting.

*Comorbidity.* The coexisting illness (physical or mental) can be managed within the same parameters as the borderline phenomena themselves. If this is not done, the illness, its symptoms or treatment, may become the vehicle through which the borderline pattern is expressed. "The symptoms you're describing to me may be caused by X, or Y, or B, or simply anxiety. I don't know which. The investigations to decide on the cause are. . . . Would you like me to order them?"

At first blush this does not appear very radical. But doctors don't usually do it this way. They usually express a clear opinion about the likely cause, and then say, "I would like to do some tests."

*Physician/Team Uncertain.* Despite reviewing the long history of admissions and pharmacological treatment and its pattern of failure, the physician still feels an adequate trial of, say, monoamine oxidase inhibitors (MAOIs) has not been conducted. The physician also doesn't believe this is possible within the relationship management approach. The therapist will likely have to wait for another failure of the traditional approach before applying this model.

*Hostility.* If the treatment team is hostile to the patient, albeit in a way that is suppressed, repressed, expiated through reaction formation, or otherwise denied, they may use the relationship management approach as a justification to reject the patient. This hostility must be addressed before relationship management is instituted.

All these principles, prerequisites, techniques, and cautions will be described in more detail, with examples, in the ensuing chapters.

# 6

# Crisis and Emergency Management

## NEW CLIENTS

Psychiatric diagnosis of a new client presenting in crisis must be tentative at best. A firm label applied at this time could be misleading or harmful. Hansell (1976) has pointed out in *The Person in Distress: Biosocial Dynamics of Adaptation*—a book that should be mandatory reading for all crisis workers—that people in distress send signals of distress (a symptom of illness might simply be a signal of distress, and a symptom of illness can be used as a signal of distress) and that people in crisis are particularly susceptible to the assignment of new identities. This is one of the reasons psychiatric hospitalization is not a benign event for anybody.

Therefore it would be unusual and perhaps dangerous to make a firm diagnosis of borderline personality disorder on a first encounter. If this is so, then on what basis can one safely apply relationship management principles to a new client?

The practical question to be asked is not, "Does the client have BPD?" but rather, "In this particular interview with this new client, is the process level of communication paramount? Is there more important meaning to be found in our interpersonal negotiations than in the events the client says brought about this state, and in the client's presentation of present distress or symptoms?"

Many experienced clinicians make this judgment very quickly. Some then act on it. Some more prudently put it aside for later consideration. What are they responding to beyond intuition or gut feeling?

> When I'm brought in to see her for the first time, she's sitting up in an infirmary bed with her newly bandaged legs. Before I'm introduced to her, she plaintively asks, "Do you think I'm hopeless, Doctor?"
> My right brain makes a prompt diagnosis. It ignores my left brain's pleas to take a proper history and do a mental status. I pause only briefly, plop myself into a chair, and say, "Probably."

The interviewer is responding to a gestalt, a pattern, and is assuming responsibility for this lies with his right brain. Using this hypothesis, he answers her question with a single word quite contrary to her expectations and quite contrary to his assigned role (in which he is expected, at the very least, to be encouraging). What exactly is he responding to, and how can he quickly test this rather cavalier hypothesis to ensure he is not being misled by prejudice, countertransference, or other nefarious artifacts?

There are several clues that indicate the interviewer might be wise to attend to the process level of communication, the interpersonal negotiation taking place at that very moment:

*Incongruity between Situation and Affect.* In this case example the client was being coy while lying in the infirmary of a psychiatric hospital. Equally suggestive are anger toward the just-now-met crisis worker, and seductive behavior.

*Exaggeration.* The display of affect or stated intent seems somewhat excessive considering the precipitating events. This is a difficult judgment to make without walking a mile in the client's shoes. Still, the manner of presentation, the choice of words (absolutes and extremes: "the most," "the worst," "is killing me," "can't . . ."), of cadence and prosody (the *worst*), of theatrical gestures (long sigh, slumping into chair) might indicate that the intended impact on the interviewer supersedes the actual experience.

*Vagueness.* Halfway through the encounter the interviewer might notice that he or she has not been able to determine what actually happened to bring about this visit or action. The affect and drama of the moment and any number of other reported events may have obscured this omission, but the interviewer has not been able to learn what actually happened to bring about this visit at this time, at least not to the extent that would satisfy the dispassionate editor looking for logic and motivation in a new screenplay.

*External Locus of Control.* When asked why she has come to the crisis center, for example, a client says her doctor sent her. When asked about her visit with the doctor, she describes going to him because of headaches, and says or implies that she doesn't know why he sent her here, or decided it was an emergency. The interviewer may let this incongruity slip by because the client's manner and language are invoking feelings of urgency.

*Effect on Listener.* The manner in which the client presents the story may create a sense of urgency in the interviewer, such as a feeling that if the interviewer doesn't respond now, and correctly, the client will walk out. The interviewer may also be assailed by images and fantasies of imminent disaster, as well as by a very strong and immediate sense of responsibility. Further, an interviewer will usually experience resentment and annoyance when "hopelessness" is being presented as an interpersonal ploy, as opposed to the feeling of sympathy engendered when "hopelessness" is an expression of a feeling state in a depressed patient.

*Assumption of Immediate Relationship.* As in the case vignette, the new client skips past etiquette, the formalities and niceties of a first encounter, the establishment of context, and the tentative warming-up phase, and engages immediately in a provocative or evocative manner: "Do you think I'm hopeless?"

*Immediate Failure.* The clinician is barely into the interview and finds himself already failing: The client says, "I don't know why I came, there's nothing you can do for me. . . . I tried that already. . . . Yes, but . . . ." This may be more subtly conveyed by the client with overt requests for suggestions and advice coupled with a tone of voice that implies very low expectations.

If some of these phenomena are present, the interviewer should suspect that the encounter, the social reality, and the outcome are being driven by the process level of communication. How can this hypothesis be quickly tested? By the interviewer's using some of the treatment dialogue techniques as tests and waiting for the *switch*. The switch refers to a shift on the part of the client from the presenting negative position to something positive, from total hopelessness and incompetence to a ray of hope, a considered action. The interview or dialogue techniques used to invoke this switch include:

1. Slowing down the interview
2. Using fewer words
3. Making use of silences
4. Responding with empathic neutrality
5. Assuming a position contrary to assigned attributes
6. Using paradoxical statements

Internal work is always necessary to deal with images, fantasies, an unreasonable sense of urgency or of foreboding responsibility, or irritation. To allow time for this internal work and time for the interviewer to ponder questions of process, the interview can be slowed down. This can be accomplished by responding more slowly, by assuming a relaxed posture, and by inserting natural breaks such as fetching coffee. The purpose of this is to ensure that the process communication is not overwhelming or controlling the interviewer.

A very common pattern of interview dialogue is one in which the interviewer's first response is a facilitating utterance ("Uh huh, I see") or empathic reflection ("It certainly sounds . . .") followed by some elaboration or modification. In the second or third phrase of elaboration, the interviewer is most likely to betray the imperatives of the interpersonal negotiation by responding to a personal need to offer hope, be clever, demonstrate competence, or maintain control. To test the hypothesis that the process level of communication is paramount, these latter phrases may be consciously withheld.

This can be an interesting exercise in itself because the interviewer can then learn to what degree he or she feels compelled to demonstrate competence.

There are comfortable silences in an interview, and there are very uncomfortable silences. The uncomfortable silences usually occur when the client has ended a statement in a manner (verbal or nonverbal) that demands a response from the interviewer, who is not forthcoming. These are the silences that can be consciously increased in number and duration to test our hypothesis. The client is left with the ownership of the last proposition, and must then respond to it. The client's choices are to repeat it, emphasize it, or modify it. It is the modification (or switch) the interviewer is waiting for.

> "Everything's hopeless."
> (silence)
> "I just can't go on anymore."
> (silence, more uncomfortable silence)
> "But I don't want to come into the hospital."
> (silence)
> "Maybe I could call my sister."

The subtext in this example has been a negotiation of responsibility and competence. The interviewer's silence has left the client to dialogue with herself. In this segment the client arrives at ownership of her positive (competent and responsible) proposition, instead of dialoguing with an active, supportive, directive therapist in such a manner that she finds she must own and defend the negative while the therapist owns and defends the positive.

The same can be achieved with responses of benign, neutral empathy, that is, empathic reflection devoid of inferences of anxiety, urgency, and responsibility. ("It does sound really bad. It does sound hopeless.").

When, in the first case vignette, the interviewer answered the question, "Do you think I'm hopeless?" with "Probably," he was responding in a manner contrary to his role or attribute assignment in the script. He was expected, in the very least, to ask with empathy if not pity, why she might feel this way, whereupon she would most certainly tell him. Or he was expected to reassure her, in which case she was amply prepared to demonstrate how misinformed he must be. She would then own and defend her position of hopelessness while he would find himself jumping linguistic hoops to cast a small ray of hope on her situation. His answer of "Probably" overturned the dialogue imperative. The client is left with a dilemma. If she is truly and seriously depressed and if she genuinely, independently of context, resides solely in a position of hopelessness, then she will perceive the interviewer's response as aloof, but she will not be compelled to counter it. On the other hand, if our hypothesis is right, and the control and relative competence negotiation is more important than her transient inner state, she will be compelled to respond. And because within this framework, the negotiation—the thrust, counterthrust, and negation of the interviewer's proposition—is more compelling than the actual position assumed, she will feel compelled to respond in a contrary manner. After all, she can achieve a sense of power, worth, and competence within her hopeless state only by demonstrating that the interviewer is even less competent and powerful, by countering his definition of the situation. Thus, if the process level of communication is paramount, she must protest his acquiescence. What she actually said, with a somewhat surprised and hurt voice, was, "You're not supposed to undermine a patient's confidence."

This is the switch. Not a bold switch, but a switch nonetheless, because she is now admitting to having confidence (read hope or competence) and suggesting that it is the doctor who might be undermining it—a very good start. He should now probably retract a little, with comments such as, "Well, I don't really know," and leave her with the decision to be hopeless or hopeful.

Some other phrases that less dramatically occupy a position contrary to the assigned attributes of power and competence include, "It does sound very messy" and "I haven't any idea what one should do in this situation" and "I don't know."

Finally, if the interviewer harbors no negative countertransference, no anger, no hatred toward and no wish to reject the client, he or she might try a true paradoxical injunction. It must be presented with a subtext of respect, with seriousness, with empathy, without a sense of challenge or threat. To the client in the first vignette, the paradoxical injunction might be presented thus: "Well, you've been admitted to the hospital 27 times, and nothing has seemed to help. And considering how much you've suffered, I'd have to conclude that it is hopeless. If I were in your shoes, I'd give up."

An important aspect of the paradox is to stop talking at this point to avoid countering, modifying, or softening what has just been said. It is this imperative that you are trying to leave with the client.

If our hypothesis is right and the process level of communication is paramount, then the *content will follow the imperatives of the process of the relationship negotiation.* This client will be compelled to counter the paradoxical injunction.

Dichotomous positions are being negotiated. Therefore, whatever the actual content—suicide, not being able to cope, not knowing what to do with self, boyfriend, hospital, job, family—if borderline phenomena are dominant, then the client, when faced with a neutral position, will vacillate from pole to pole, and switch to the opposite pole when the therapist assumes a contrary position.

In practice this may mean empathically but neutrally following a client down through increasing protestations of hopelessness and incompetence, until, following the interviewer's silence, the client switches, and offers tentatively some positive action he or she might engage in. At this point the therapist should remain neutral—or even doubtful—and let the client build up to the other side.

## KNOWN PATIENTS

With a client we know well to have a borderline personality disorder presenting in crisis, the therapist or crisis worker will likely have several questions uppermost in mind:

1. Is this presentation different? Does it represent "real" illness (e.g., depression) this time?
2. Do the circumstances (stresses, precipitating events) this time warrant a protective response?
3. How can hospitalization be avoided safely?

4. If I must hospitalize the client, how can I ensure that the experience is not regressive and counterproductive?

If the new illness is physical, it can be responded to in the usual manner within a traditional social contract. It may not become a vehicle used in the distorting interpersonal negotiation. If it does become currency in a negotiation of control or competence, the therapist can revert quickly to the stance of relationship management:

> "That cut looks really deep. It may need stitches. We should get the emergency intern to have a look at it."
> "I'm not going near any goddamn doctors."
> "OK, it's up to you. It's your decision."
> "He'll want to put me in the hospital."
> "Yeah, he might."
> "Well, I'm not going into the hospital."
> "No. Not if you don't want to."
> "Do you think it needs stitches?"
> "It might reduce the size of the scar you're going to have. But it's up to you."

If the seemingly new problem is a mental illness (severe depression, a psychotic symptom), the crisis therapist/physician can resolve the dilemma by reframing the questions. Instead of the question, "Is this a true mood disorder this time?" the more useful questions are, "How can I safely find out if antidepressants would benefit the client, and if they would be helpful, how can I get the client to take them without their becoming troublesome currency in our interpersonal negotiation?"

First of all, the question of depression probably arose too early and urgently. As these patients tend to evoke a sense of urgency in the situation, we are prone to look for something solid we can treat ("At last, a real illness with a real pill I can prescribe. Thank God."). If the stance and techniques of relationship management as described above and throughout the book are utilized, the question of a "treatable depression" may evaporate. The appearance of slowness, flattened affect, depressed mood, reduced energy, and suicidal ideation may shift within the one interview to a broader range of affect, normal speech patterns, energy, and statements of positive intent. The question has then been answered for the moment.

If this does not happen, then the therapist should reframe the question as above. It should also be remembered that this borderline patient is probably well acquainted with the medications used in the treatment of depression as well as the symptoms and signs of the illness; and knows what has helped or not helped or made him or her worse in the past. It should also be acknowledged that the accurate diagnosis of a mood disorder is irrelevant unless the patient makes use of, and responds well to treatment. With the question reframed, it is clear that diagnostic certainty is an indulgence in this case. We really simply want to find a way of safely helping the patient. This can be done by discussing the use of antidepressants strictly within the guidelines of relationship management:

> "You seem very depressed today."
> "I've never felt worse.
> "Have you ever taken antidepressants?"
> "They didn't do me any good."
> "What ones did you take?"
> "I don't know. Etrafon and Tofranil."
> "There are quite a few others."
> "Do you think I should take one?"
> "I don't know. There's drug X. It might help you. Of course there are side effects with every drug."
> "Yeah, just what I need. Blurred vision, dry mouth."
> "Well, it's up to you. The dosage would likely be . . . the benefits might be . . . the side effects might be . . . and it would take about 10 days to begin working."
> "You think I should try it?"
> "I don't know. It might help. It might not. And the side effects might be intolerable. I really don't know if it would help or not. You'll have to decide. I'll prescribe some for you if you want me to."

You'll notice we haven't mentioned the possibility of hospitalization for "further testing and observation" with respect to the possibility of mood disorder. This is a spurious rationale for hospital-ization and should be avoided. After "testing and observation," the question remains the same: "Does the client benefit from one of the known treatments for mood disorder, and how can it be prescribed so that it doesn't become troublesome currency in our interpersonal negotiations?"

The question of whether the current stresses or precipitating events ever constitute a reason for a more protective response has a short answer: "No, but there must be exceptions."

She was a very troublesome patient. She'd actually been diag-nosed as schizophrenic and placed in a schizophrenia rehabil-itation program. She overdosed on an irregular basis and tantalized interns and psychiatric residents with her bizarre genital mutilation fantasies, which they undoubtedly reported to their supervisors, who nodded wisely. When we took her on and applied what we now call relationship management, it worked. There was one more overdose followed by our state-ment that "we do not prescribe pills to people who abuse them. You can get them elsewhere but not from this clinic." Then she settled in and told us how she had adopted various psychotic symptoms while in the psychiatric hospital, and how she elab-orated her fantasies to please her various past therapists. She attended courses in child care and landed a job. Through all of this, she struggled with her rather ambivalent relationship with her mother. She attended her new outpatient therapist faithfully, bringing each time a small offering of food or drink. Then her mother died, quite suddenly, and she came in and told us this.

Of course we considered this a major emotional event and ample reason to drop the strict relationship management approach and offer more empathy and concern. This we did, and she became more weepy and concerned for her safety. We offered more empathy and a protective response, and she became more incompetent. She was grieving and it began to seem that the only safe place for her was in the hospital. And then it occurred to us, in line with one of the tenets of relation-ship management, that healthy, competent adults do not usually require psychiatric hospitalization upon the loss of a loved one. In fact, there are undoubtedly far more reasonable contexts in which to grieve.

So we returned to relationship management, she became increasingly competent (though still grieving), and did not require hospitalization.

The point here is that even when the new stress is severe, and empathically we respond to it, the interpersonal negotiation continues. Our deeper or renewed empathy leads to distortions, or to the rekindling of our old excessively protective, rescuing, and ultimately disabling role position. At this time it is important to remember one of the principles of relationship management: The client is an intelligent, competent adult. Then ask the questions: Could an intelligent, competent adult cope with this situation? With appropriate help? With someone to talk to? Even in such a way as to eventually grow or learn from the experience?

There must be human experiences so stressful that even an intelligent, competent adult might best be put in a hospital bed and sedated for 48 hours. However, they aren't common clinical situations.

From a practical crisis management perspective, this proposition can be quickly tested. The therapist feels compelled to offer a more protective response (concern, questions implying responsibility, suggestions, advice). If this induces an even greater display of helplessness and hopelessness, then clearly it was the wrong thing to do. The therapist can then correct, as in the case example, and revert to the style of relationship management, which does not preclude attentiveness, respect, and empathy.

Even for health professionals not steeped in these and related ideas, it may become apparent that hospitalization is not helpful for certain borderline patients. We are slow to learn, and this may not occur to us until the 5th, 12th, or 18th hospitalization. Even then we can find many professionals rationalizing this counterproductive pattern by declaring that the client may need frequent short hospitalizations for the rest of his or her life. It should also be noted that when we think these patients have been, for example, seen in emergency eight times and hospitalized 10 times, we probably know only half the story. In a study of multiservice users (Finlayson et al., 1983), many of whom would be diagnosed borderline, an important observation not reported was that far more hospital events were found to have occurred than the current care givers had been aware of.

When treatment teams do come to the conclusion that either further hospitalization will not help, or will be harmful, rudimentary attempts to preclude further hospitalization are invoked. We use the term "rudimentary" because usually these first attempts are actually disguised rejections, the acting out of a wish for this patient to go away. A note is sent to the crisis team suggesting this patient not be admitted again, and when they do call to obtain admission, the intake worker tells them, "No way." So they wait until the intake worker is off duty and seek admission through another staff member, or the patient displays more convincing currency, or the patient gets admitted to another hospital, which may then call up the next day requesting transfer.

The point of avoiding hospitalization is not rejection. In fact, rejecting a borderline patient usually leads to one of two consequences: The rejection becomes the stimulus for an advance in the repertoire, the currency used in the next negotiation with the same therapist or institution, or it constitutes the natural end point of the distorted dialogue (therapist proved to be uncaring, incompetent; patient most powerful in unlovable helplessness) and time for the patient to move on to another therapist, another system.

There may be some instances when this kind of rejection has a good outcome (as in the unintended paradoxical injunction by the senior resident who told his patient she was a hopeless, untreatable personality disorder). A good outcome may occur when patients are thus provoked into proving they don't need therapy/help or when they move on to dialogue with a more benign helping agency. In fact, in the early stages of the development of relationship management, one clinic introduced the practice of "*depsychiatrization*" for patients with speckled histories of self-destructive behavior and repeated hospitalizations (see previous chapter). This constituted a relationship management approach in which a primary goal was to gently shift the patient's care away from the medical/psychiatric environment (with its dangerous currency) to that of a social agency, with backup and support from psychiatry—from "patient" to "client," perhaps to empowered client or self-help agent.

But repeated regressive hospitalizations can be avoided within a broader care plan. This is obviously easier within a system or network of services, where the crisis team and inpatient, day care, and outpatient therapists can work together. The first step is the case conference, with each service or agency represented. This always appears to be a very expensive endeavor, but when considered against the repeated admissions and often unbridled use of services, it is ultimately more economical when it works.

The difference between a multiservice case conference with most clients and that held for a borderline client is simply that the principles of relationship management should be enacted in the very organization and prosecution of the conference. The team may need a preliminary meeting to get this straight, but once in the main conference, relationship management should be enacted. What does this mean in a conference setting? This means the client will have approved of all attending, may have supplied a list, and may have even set up the conference. For an outpatient multiservice user, the client can be asked whom he or she would like to attend, and asked if he or she would like to be the one to invite them. A client who is at all worried about sitting in a room with six to a dozen personnel from health and social agencies may invite a friend or advocate. For a predischarge conference from a ward, the inpatient service can assume a little control over the list of participants.

At the conference, after introductions, one person, the leader, sets the stage, describes the purpose of the meeting, but within the style of relationship management. In this presentation the leader briefly reviews the past, always looking to the client for correction or modification, and does so using straightforward honest language:

> "Well, as we all know—now correct me if I get any of this wrong, Joan—Joan has been hospitalized, how many? 12 times. Sometimes voluntarily but usually involuntarily—is that right, Joan? And for the most part we haven't been of much help to her."
>
> "Gives me time to get my head together," Joan says.

"OK, but our pills haven't helped much, and usually the admissions end up involving seclusion room and locked end, and the admissions usually come about because either Joan tells someone in the emergency department she's suicidal or she overdoses . . . and it keeps happening and we don't know what to do . . . Joan doesn't usually want to come into the hospital so she gets certified . . . so we've called this meeting to put our heads together, because we haven't done much good up to now, and to see if there's any better way to help Joan and to ask Joan herself what she thinks we should do when next time she's upset and calls the crisis service and tells them she's suicidal. And at the same time ask Joan herself what she would like in the way of help from any of the people around this table. For instance, when you leave the hospital, do you want to see a therapist and how often . . . and what would you like that therapist to do?"

Now, when Joan starts telling the various professionals around the table what she would like from them, they have to be very honest and clear—for example, "I'm afraid I can see you only once a week, Joan, that's all the time I have."

The leader of the conference must lead the discussion to the past and inevitable future crises. For example, in answer to Joan's saying, "I'm all right this time," the leader might respond, "OK, but just in case you take an overdose of pills and you're brought to the emergency, what would you like us to do? I mean beyond doing what we have to do medically if you're unconscious or really sick, I mean after that?"

Here we need faith. And this faith is usually rewarded. Borderline patients, like other competent adults, usually make good choices for themselves when they are not being driven along by a distorted interpersonal negotiation. If this has been handled well, Joan is likely to tell us either "I just need someone to talk to for awhile and then be allowed to go home" or "Sometimes I need to be in the hospital, or crisis housing, for a couple of days. Just a couple of days, though."

At the end of the conference, the leader can sum up the new social contract, the new plan, getting at the same time further agreement and approval from Joan. Joan has designed her own aftercare and her own crisis response service. The answer we're looking for with respect to managing crises is the "I just need someone to talk to, and then decide what I'm going to do myself and go home." This becomes then the basis for the new social contract, overt and agreed upon, between the various agencies and Joan. "What if you're still saying you feel suicidal? What should we do then? Should we force you into the hospital?"

At this point the leader may need to dialogue extensively with Joan to make sure she is the one to decide these issues. She will probably tell us never to hospitalize her when she wants to go home.

Finally, this becomes the background social contract. To enact it, however, the outpatient therapist and the crisis therapist need to know how to apply relationship management in their crisis interviews, using the same techniques described with new patients in crisis plus the other outpatient techniques. To achieve this may require that one designated person always be called when this patient goes into crisis. This may appear an onerous task, but if carried out correctly, the number of times the patient goes into crisis should diminish to extinction.

Now if Joan tells us instead that there are times when she feels so bad she will want to come into the hospital, and so requests that each time she comes into emergency she be admitted to a particular doctor's team, the team is likely to recoil defensively. We are feeding into her dependency, they will say. But this isn't how it works. According to the concepts outlined in this book, she is not seeking dependency or attention. She is seeking the re-creation of the distorted interpersonal negotiations. In her interviews with the crisis worker, this has been taking the following form of:

*Joan:* I'm incompetent, helpless.

*Crisis Worker:* Come into the hospital. We'll take care of you.

*Joan:* I don't want to come in.

*Crisis Worker:* Will you be all right then?

*Joan:* No, I'm going to kill myself.

*Crisis Worker:* I insist you come in . . . .

When we no longer participate in this tussle, she will no longer need it. When she is given choice and access to both coming into and leaving the hospital, the distorted dialogue has ended and she will not need further hospitalizations.

Of course, it's not always this smooth. She may still find a crisis worker to engage in the distorted dialogue with her, maybe telling her she can't or shouldn't go into the hospital, or a hospital intake worker who heard the words of the care plan, but not the music, and withholds admission, or takes the next request for admission as obvious incompetence on the part of the patient or the consultant who advised this plan in the first place.

What we do guarantee is that the point for these patients is not hospitalization, not satisfying dependency needs, but rather reengaging in the pathological interpersonal negotiation. If this is stopped, if the distorted dialogue is stopped, the patient's requests for hospitalization will cease.

And only if the inpatient team is willing and able to apply these principles can the admitting crisis worker be ensured that this admission will not be regressive and counterproductive.

# 7

# Inpatient Management

It should be clear by now that the authors do not favor inpatient treatment of borderline personality disorder. The previous chapter outlined some techniques for preventing such admissions. However, people with this problem do regularly find their way to inpatient services in general hospitals, and psychiatric hospitals. Some hospitals offer special programs for people with personality disorder. These range from intensive psychotherapy within a holding environment to some form of therapeutic community (Tucker et al., 1987; Eppel, 1988; Gabbard, 1986).

From experience with therapeutic communities in the 1960s and early 1970s, the authors would conclude that if people with borderline or other personality disorders are to reside in hospital wards for any length of time, a well-run sophisticated therapeutic community might be the safest of various models. In a true therapeutic community, virtually all decisions affecting all people, staff and patients alike, are made by group consensus, after, of course, interminable discussion. The hierarchy is flattened, power shifts to the collective, decisions are made by vote or consensus, communication channels multiply. In a good therapeutic community, sapiential authority replaces role authority. Of course, most therapeutic communities achieve only partial flattening, with much power and many decisions remaining with the staff alone. Psychotherapies, pharmacotherapies, and rehabilitation activities can occur in a therapeutic community as in any other hospital service. The real difference is twofold. Patients are transformed into responsible decision-making adults, true "self-care agents" *in control of and responsible for* their own treatment, successes, and failures, and social control is achieved through the establishment of group norms, group pressure, and group sanction. These groups uniformly seem better able to distinguish a genuine suicidal wish from an interpersonal negotiation than do many individual health care professionals. They can be effective in creating an environment in which someone with a borderline personality appears to act badly less often, acquire self-system stability, and perhaps gain some self-esteem from helping others. It should be noted that the social contract implicit in a therapeutic community contains many of the elements of the relationship management social contract.

However, therapeutic communities tend to be medium- to long-stay units (some consistency is necessary to attain group norms and group means for enforcing those norms), and require a very special commitment from the leader and the staff. They are expensive, rare, and tend to have limited life spans. They are very dependent on a charismatic leader, and they are usually regarded with suspicion by the rest of the hospital. A further problem for therapeutic communities is the broader psychiatric literature that clearly indicates that longer periods of hospitalization hamper all ex-patients' return to social and vocational roles, and that what a patient learns in a special environment may not transfer to the normal community (Mattes, 1982). So therapeutic communities are not a rational answer for the vast majority of borderlines who are or may be hospitalized. And the many destructive events that can befall a borderline hospitalized on a regular ward have already been addressed.

Relationship management can help get a borderline patient through a hospitalization with minimal chaos and regression and, perhaps occasionally, with some benefit. It can also eliminate repeated admissions, overturn some long-standing messy situations, and prevent the kind of no-win struggles that happen all too often.

Some of these patients are straightforward, and the timely (immediately upon admission) application of relationship management can ensure a brief, untroubled, and perhaps productive inpatient experience. Some other patients present more long-standing complex problems with which the application of relationship management requires considerable work, negotiation, inventiveness, and a more gradual period of bringing the situation under control.

It can be difficult to institute relationship management on an inpatient service, but the factors that make it so do not usually reside within the patient.

## THE CONTRACT

The essential feature of inpatient management of the borderline patient is the social contract. This can be a written contract, but it need not be, for it is a very simple contract. It can also be signed by the patient and staff, but it need not be, especially if the patient balks. The signing or refusal to sign a contract must not become another vehicle for distorted negotiations. The relationship management contract does *not* include a list of things the patient promises to do, as in a common kind of inpatient contract in which the patient promises to get up in the morning, go to occupational therapy, attend group, stay on the ward between 9 and 12, and so on. This is contrary to the contract struck in relationship management because it begs to be tested, and places policing of these behaviors in the hands of the staff. And what are the sanctions? Reprimands? Discussion? That kind of contract merely gives the pathological dialogue new vehicles for negotiation. By contrast, the contract that should be struck with every borderline patient will contain the following elements:

- Voluntary status only.
- Length of stay discussed and negotiated at outset.
- Full privileges always, no restrictions.
- Patient chooses activities and programs.
- Patient chooses to go or not to go to these programs.
- Standard, routine observation no matter what patient does.
- Patient may discharge self anytime.
- Patient will set own goals.
- Patient will tell staff what he or she wishes from them.
- Staff will honestly tell patient whether or not they can comply with patient's wishes.
- Patient will decide on own medication—type, form, and

dose—with information from staff, verbal and written, and clear limits.

- Staff will give patient information.
- Staff will explicitly explain any absolute boundaries (e.g., barbiturates are never prescribed; the upper limit of antidepressant X is 250 milligrams per day).
- Patient will decide if any investigations are to be carried out, after staff have explained the purpose, potential value, and potential negative effects.
- Staff clearly delineate those behaviors that will bring about immediate discharge: These usually include aggression, intoxication, self-mutilation, suicidal behavior, and interfering with other patients. Anything else that a given ward cannot tolerate can be added to this list. Only that which honestly cannot be tolerated should be forbidden and backed up with immediate discharge. Immediate discharge, sometimes with legal charges, is the only therapeutic response to aggression, violence, and interfering with other patients.

  In certain circumstances, discussed later, a response of "nothing will happen, nothing will change" can be used for intoxication, self-mutilation, and suicidal behavior.

In straightforward cases this social contract is explained and discussed with the patient upon admission, or at least right after initial interviews are complete. Most borderline patients then choose to stay a few days to a couple of weeks, and the admission proceeds without incident. A psychiatrist who must immediately discharge one patient for behaviors listed above will probably not have to discharge another in similar circumstances for many months. The patient culture learns this is no idle threat from this particular team and this particular psychiatrist.

At the time of the contract, and throughout the admission, the therapist, psychiatrist, primary nurse, and, to whatever extent possible, all other staff, dialogue with the patient using the stance and techniques previously discussed to ensure the social contract is not undermined. Most staff are instructed to redirect the patient to the therapist, psychiatrist, or primary nurse if the request or conversation deviates from immediate and simple concerns.

There is a kind of contracting that is very common that should *never* be used with a borderline patient. "Promise me that if you feel like cutting your wrists or overdosing you will first talk with a nurse and tell her about your feelings and intentions" (so we can prevent you from doing it). This is entirely contrary to relationship management. It reinforces the notion that the patient is an incompetent, impulse-driven organism, not in control. It also multiplies the potential for distorted dialogues. Now *we* are responsible for the patient's behavior and control of that behavior. With this kind of contract, the patient may or may not talk to the nurse beforehand, and may or may not claim to have tried and failed to find a nurse before doing the deed (our fault). If the patient talks to the nurse, one of two outcomes is possible: Having talked with the nurse, the patient states that he or she is no longer suicidal and goes off (and repeats the next day), or having talked with the nurse, the patient says he or she is still suicidal and the nurse must then institute closer observation and/or control. The dialogue continues with self-harm verbalization as major transactional currency.

Besides the "tell us before you harm yourself" contract, another common inpatient pattern is to establish a contract that details the circumstances in which the patient may seek voluntary seclusion, voluntary restraints, and voluntary p.r.n. medication and the circumstances in which the staff will enforce seclusion, restraints, and medication. This is contrary to relationship management and, in our view, simply institutionalizes a pattern of distorting and regressive negotiations.

The firm belief underlying the relationship management social contract is that the patient is an intelligent adult, responsible for actions and decisions, and to treat the patient otherwise, overtly or covertly, is destructive.

When the principles of relationship management are applied in an inpatient setting they translate as follows: *The patient is an intelligent, responsible adult.* The team meets with the patient as early as possible, and the new social contract is presented and discussed. As listed above, it includes, "You are voluntary and always will be voluntary, no matter what happens, or what you do. You have full privileges, and these will not be restricted no matter what you do. You decide how long you would like to stay, and you decide which medications you want and which programs you attend. You will not be under special observation. We'll give you whatever information we have on these things, but you will make the decisions."

Of course this has been presented here in precis form. The actual dialogue may go something like this:

"You mean you'd just let me go if I wanted?"

"Yes. It's up to you. You've been in the hospital a few times before. Only *you* know whether it helps or not."

"I don't believe this. You doctors never agree on anything. Dr. Matthews told me I had to come into the hospital and I had to stay for a while. So you're saying he doesn't know what he's doing."

"No. I'm saying I don't know. I guess that was his opinion at the time."

"So you don't agree with it. You think I don't need to be here."

"No. I'm not saying that. I'm saying I don't know whether you should stay or not. It's up to you to decide."

"I can't believe this. You'd just let me walk outa here?"

"Yes, if you wanted to."

"Even when I'm suicidal?"

"Well, that's up to you, too. You can stay if you think it would help, or you could go home now. And whether or not you harm yourself has always been in your own hands and always will be. We have no actual power to stop your killing or hurting yourself if that's what you really want to do." This dialogue would continue until the patient clearly decides whether to stay or go. If the patient finally decides to stay the next question is:

"How long would you like to stay? A week, 2 weeks?"

"Maybe a week."

"OK. So we could plan your discharge for when? Before next weekend or for Monday?"

"Monday."

If there are specific length-of-stay restrictions for this ward or insurance limitations, these are matter of factly presented to the patient.

Borderline inpatients are not treated like other patients within the traditional social contract of the medical model. They are told that virtually all decisions are in their hands, and the therapist and other staff dialogue with them using the skills already outlined to ensure that this decision making remains theirs. This applies to all areas of their hospitalization: Programs are described to them and they decide to attend or not; programs are not promoted. The answer to the question, "Do you think it would help?" is "I don't know." Medications are discussed with them in great detail, both past medications and possible new medications. The potential positive effects are described along with the potential side effects. The difference between this and the process of informed consent that should occur with all patients is that with borderline patients the psychiatrist and nurses will *not suggest, recommend, or promote* any of the medications. The patients will decide without influence. As in all situations with borderline patients, this is not a simple matter. Achieving the goal of a patient's actually deciding without influence or perceived influence from the psychiatrist requires utilization of the dialogue techniques described in the previous chapter. The nonverbal must be attended to:

"All right," she says, "I'll take the Prozac."
If the "all right" has a tone of giving in, and the "take" has a sense of willingness under protest, the psychiatrist must immediately respond to this rather than accepting the apparent decision:
"Now I want to be clear about this. I'm not recommending the Prozac. I don't know whether it would help or not. It helps some people, others it doesn't."
"So you don't think I should take it?"
"No, I'm not saying that either. I'm saying I don't know. It's up to you."
At this point she may shift to an attack on the psychiatrist's competence, and he must resist defending himself:

"You're the doctor. Aren't you supposed to know these things?"

This would be a good moment to apply the technique of adopting the *posture of the natural end point* of such a dialogue by agreeing: "Well, maybe some doctors think they know the answers to this question, but I don't. In fact, there's a chance the medication will do more harm than good. I really don't know."

Within this *apparently* laissez-faire but actually honest dialogue about medication, clear limits can be set in a matter-of-fact manner: "Drug X is addictive and I never prescribe it." "I never prescribe drug X and drug Y together." "The highest recommended dose of drug W is 20 milligrams per day. I can give you up to that but no more." "If you abuse the pills I prescribe, I won't prescribe any more pills for you."

## Limit Setting

The most important limit is the ward response to self-mutilative behavior, suicidal behavior, aggression, and intoxication. Traditional responses to these behaviors can be discussed at great length. But within the social contract of relationship management, only two possible responses exist. These are *immediate discharge* and the understanding that *absolutely nothing will happen, nothing will change*. Any other response to these behaviors occurring in a hospital ward leads to collusion in the pathological interpersonal negotiation underlying the behavior, and a reinforcement of these behaviors as legitimate currency. These sanctions must be clear and absolute. Ambivalence, equivocation, and half measures will also reinforce the behaviors.

The simplest and most effective response, which is presented to the patient in the entry social contract discussion, is immediate discharge. Although a regular ward might use this sanction for intoxication and/or aggression, it is unlikely to be invoked for suicidal behavior. However, when this is presented to the patient upon admission, it is seldom if ever tested. To ensure it is carried out if necessary, the attending psychiatrist must be willing to be called at home and/or document and sign instructions for discharge should certain events happen. If the infraction (e.g., wrist cutting) occurs at night, it is sufficient to discharge the patient first thing in the morning, but no later. When a patient needs to be discharged in this manner, the patient and outpatient therapist can be told that a readmission is possible and can be applied for, but the same rules would apply. Fortunately, as mentioned above, the psychiatrist and treatment team may have to follow through only once with one patient because from that point on this new social contract will be well appreciated by the patient culture. The news spreads quickly.

> "One of the very strict rules we have on this ward is that should you engage in suicidal or self-destructive behavior of any kind, such as wrist cutting and overdosing, you will be immediately discharged."
> "Yeah, I heard about that."

In the presentation of this sanction to the patient, all likely behaviors must be mentioned. The borderline patient will look for loopholes in the social contract.

> This social contract was eventually presented to one of the young men discussed in the chapter on adolescents, which is to follow. He would be immediately discharged if he cut himself, burned himself, or swallowed things. That very night a nurse asked him if he would like ice cream. He asked, "Do you think the doctor would count starving myself as suicidal behavior?"
> The nurse answered, "Yes."
> "In that case," said the boy, "I'll have some ice cream."

Another patient was told earlier that she would be immediately discharged if she overdosed (her usual behavior), but cutting was not mentioned. That evening she cut herself. When confronted and told she would be discharged, she said, "But you didn't mention wrist slashing."
So it is wise, when stating the contract, to be overinclusive.

## Boundaries

If the hospitalization is short (a few days, one week), concern about *same-sex therapists* will not be so great. Private distortions can be avoided by an expectation of full disclosure and full discussion at team meetings. There are no private sessions. This can be presented to the patient, with the principal team members in attendance, simply as, "This is the way we work." The length of time and time of day this patient sees the primary nurse or therapist is specified and adhered to. Still, with borderline patients one of three things happens all too frequently despite our vigilance:

1. The young male psychiatry resident schedules his appointments with the female patient for 5 P.M., the sessions last longer than 1 hour, and they often take walks on the grounds. At team meetings this is omitted from his report. Some of the nurses know about this, gossip about it, but don't mention it in the formal team meeting.
2. The female borderline patient is readmitted. One of the male nurses seems quite perturbed by this. It turns out that he has been dating her between her hospitalizations.
3. The ward team has the situation under control. They have struck a good contract with the patient, but reluctantly they have agreed to let the patient continue to see her psychologist/therapist off the ward during her hospitalization. The psychologist has agreed to report on his sessions to the team. The patient agrees. Two weeks in a row the psychologist has failed to attend a team meeting, it seems the patient is now seeing him three times a week, and the nurses are wondering what's going on in his office. A differential dialogue (splitting) has begun.

All of this speaks to the need for constant vigilance during the hospitalization of a borderline patient. Boundaries must be set and maintained. Communication must be full and honest. Distortions must be detected and corrected. To do otherwise is harmful to the patient. Of course, to do this the entire treatment team must be cohesive, not suffer from internal conflict arising from discipline, role, or personality, and have strong leadership. This is asking a great deal of a modern multidisciplinary inpatient team. When doubts arise a consultation should be requested.

## Goals

Within the social contract, the staff's goal is simply to do no harm. Patients may have other goals. In the discussion/negotiations about admission, patients will be asked for their goals during their stay. The team will avoid all attempts on the part of patients to get them to express expectations, advice, direction (other than the setting of absolute boundaries around aggression, intoxication, and suicidal behavior). They will also avoid all the usual reassurances: "This is the best place for you." "We can help you with. . . ." Patients instead will be asked what they would like to accomplish during the hospitalization and how they think this might come about. What do they want and expect from the staff? During the answer, the interviewer will guide the patient to concrete and specific requests, and the team will quite matter of factly say whether or not they can actually fulfill those requests. When the expectation is that the staff will make or help patients feel better, be happy, be conflict free, feel better about themselves, the team will say they don't know how to do that. Does the patient have any ideas how they could do this? Well, the patient says, it might help if I could talk to a nurse every day. This the team can deliver.

The point is not the actual goals set by the patient. The point is that at the end of this intake dialogue, the patient will have decided whether to stay or not to stay and also what for, and be in control of the manner in which he or she might achieve the goals. Distortions and unrealistic expectations will have been stifled. The stage is set. It is now possible that the admission will be uneventful, short, helpful, yet not encouraging future admissions. Besides, this is the actual therapy: In making his or her own decisions, the patient has exercised the competent, responsible side of the self-system conflict in a healthy rather than an oppositional manner.

However, in many cases this initial striking of the social contract forms a backdrop for further interpersonal negotiations.

Judy was readmitted again to the consternation of the inpatient staff. Her outpatient therapist had, on a Friday afternoon (never schedule appointments with borderline patients for Friday afternoon), succumbed to her suicide communication and ordered her once again into the hospital. In the initial dialogue, much time was taken discussing whether she would stay or leave. In fact, her answer to the question, "Has being in the hospital ever helped before?" was "No." She then attempted to split the outpatient psychiatrist with the inpatient team, trying to get them to say the outpatient psychiatrist was wrong to send her in. The inpatient psychiatrist didn't know if the outpatient psychiatrist was right or wrong—only she, Judy, might know.

She decided to stay. The next issue was a medication, an MAOI, the outpatient psychiatrist had started her on. It caused her many side effects. The dialogue over its benefits versus its drawbacks took a good half hour. Judy used all the verbal and nonverbal skills at her disposal to get the inpatient psychiatrist to decide for her. He would know when he had inadvertently leaned one way or the other, or been perceived to lean one way or the other, because she would immediately mount counterarguments.

In fact the dialogue around the MAOI continued for a few days. When this settled, her length of stay became an issue. It seemed she sensed that though staff had left the length of stay up to her, they preferred a shorter admission. She procrastinated on picking a discharge date for herself. Apparent physical illnesses got in the way and/or became currency in the negotiation. It was discovered the family doctor attending the ward was investigating her for possible angina and heart disease, though she was a nonsmoker in her early thirties. (If possible, the family doctor should be involved and aware, but not all such variables can be controlled. If it can't be controlled, it should be ignored.)

The dialogue that had not come to closure remained an interpersonal negotiation around control and responsibility. The staff were doing things for her, deciding things for her and failing. She said being in the hospital made her worse. Staff agreed. She stayed.

This impasse was finally broken with one extensive interview utilizing the more extreme techniques of relationship management. Up to this point the inpatient stance had been one of benign neutrality. In this final encounter the interviewer adopted the end point position and ensured that there were long silences, that he said as little as possible, and that he utilized some postures contrary to expectation. This meant an opening statement of failure:

"We haven't helped you."

"I'm no better."

"I agree."

"Should I . . ."

"I haven't any idea." (The interviewer's tone and posture reflect the content of his statements.)

"I might as well be home."

(silence)

"I'm still suicidal."

(silence)

"Those pills keep me up all night."

(silence)

"This place stinks."

"Yeah. It's a pretty rotten environment."

"I think it makes me worse."

"It makes a lot of people worse."

(This cannot be rushed. Patients will eventually switch, but will reach this at their own pace.)

In the end Judy decided to stop the medication and to let her own family doctor decide about her heart later, and set a discharge date for herself 2 days hence. Unfortunately, shortly after discharge she fired her then-current outpatient psychiatrist and found another with whom she could engage in a pathological interpersonal negotiation, this next time with misuse of lithium as currency. (This unfortunate outcome, moving on to a therapist who will willingly collude in the iatrogenic process, will be discussed in the next chapter.)

## COMMAND HALLUCINATIONS

A command hallucination is a symptom of psychotic illness, usually schizophrenia. Or is it always? One justification for remaining with the diagnosis of borderline personality disorder in the presence of reported hallucinations is to include minipsychotic symptoms in the criteria for BPD (George & Soloff, 1986; Widiger et al., 1986; Widiger & Frances, 1989) However, the command hallucinations as reported by a schizophrenic are fundamentally different from those reported by someone with BPD. It has been suggested by Pope and colleagues (1985) that the psychotic features observed among patients with borderline personality disorder may be factitious—under voluntary control.

The hallucinations of someone with schizophrenia may derive directly from autonomous brain activity. Another possibility is that they arise secondarily to a failure of external sensory input and internal organization, in a manner related to the hallucinations experienced in sensory deprivation. The content, of course, is influenced by personal and cultural factors. This is not to say that someone suffering from schizophrenia will not learn to use autonomous experiences as negotiating currency with mental health workers. Every sophisticated crisis worker knows that when a chronic schizophrenic walks into the crisis center and says the voices are saying to commit suicide, the crisis worker should then ask if the client has run out of money and when the next welfare check comes. In this sense the schizophrenic is behaving in a borderline fashion in that the process-level interpersonal negotiation is more important than the actual but unknowable true internal experience of hallucinations.

The schizophrenic has voices and may learn to use them. The borderline probably learns to use them and then has them. By this we mean that the first statement of hallucinations to the staff by a borderline patient is a *proposition*, probably not an internal reality. Depending on the psychiatrist's and staff's reaction, the presence of hallucinations will or will not become a social reality and powerful currency in the ensuing negotiations. Does the patient actually hear these things? Is he or she lying? These questions are nonstarters if indeed borderline phenomena are dominant and are being managed as interpersonal negotiations. But perhaps the best way to think about such symptoms as presented by someone with BPD is with an understanding of the extent to which all experience is socially constructed and socially defined. That is, if a young female patient proposes that voices told her to cut her legs, and if we accept this as reality and give it great credence in our ensuing negotiations about power and control, she will probably come to believe it is, in fact, true. We have collaborated in the creation of a social reality.

A seriously ill acute schizophrenic does not present hallucinations as negotiation currency. The patient is usually reluctant to confess such experience, and when cajoled into doing so, does so in a detached, distracted manner. By contrast, a person with BPD usually presents the proposition of command hallucinations in a context and manner that are very engaging, very interpersonal.

> The possibly psychotic, possibly personality-disordered patient hit another patient who had changed the TV channel. When the psychiatrist questioned him about this aggression, the patient said, "God told me to do it."
>
> "No, it couldn't have been God," said the psychiatrist. "God wouldn't tell somebody to hit somebody else. It must have been the devil. I'll bet it was the devil told you to do it."
>
> "Yeah," said the patient. "It must have been the devil."
>
> "No," said the psychiatrist. "On second thought it couldn't have been the devil. He doesn't mix in this kind of thing. It was probably all the other people in the room. They were probably thinking it, and you heard their thoughts."
>
> The patient hesitated this time, but then agreed, "Yeah, they were telling me to do it."
>
> The psychiatrist, sure of his diagnosis now, said, "Look, you hit him because he turned the channel. And if you do anything like this again, any violence or aggression of any kind, I will immediately discharge you."

## PROCESS NEGOTIATIONS

An outpatient setting is liable to be psychodynamic and interpretive. An inpatient setting is usually medical. Thus, in most inpatient settings, behaviors are symptoms, patterns of behavior are syndromes. Cutting one's wrists or hitting another patient means "poor impulse control"; doing it more than once means "episodic dyscontrol syndrome." Within relationship management, however cutting and hitting are clearly not perceived as evidence of inadequate internal control mechanisms. They are perceived as illicit currency and must be disqualified as legitimate currency in interpersonal negotiations. This does not deny the possible reality of a borderline patient who does have damaged or poorly developed neurological internal control mechanisms. It is simply that the interpersonal level of interpretation is dominant. Even so, within relationship management, the more practical question, "Would either neuroleptic medication or anticonvulsant medication help?" can be addressed:

> "You've been on neuroleptics before, and you say they don't help. Well, there is another drug, an antiseizure drug that some of the experts say helps with impulse control in some cases. I don't know whether it would help you or not. The side effects are. . . . If it worked, it would presumably reduce the number of times you hit somebody else. I can give you literature on the drug if you'd like. Let me know what you think and if you'd like to try it or not."

Whatever basic interpersonal negotiation is being played out between this patient and others will be enacted around this issue as with all others. The process is constant. The vigilance required to change this process must be equally constant. The patient who has assumed a helpless, incompetent stance is liable to respond to the above presentation with, "I don't know, how am I to know, you're the doctor, do you think it would help?" or a negative as a prompter for the positive: "I've heard about that medication. It makes your hair fall out." The physician is then expected to deny the hair problem, defend the medication, and thus be, covertly at least, recommending it.

If the negotiation is around control, then the patient is liable to respond with, "All right, I'll try it if you want me to" or "No bloody way I'm taking that. I don't have epilepsy." Each of these statements is designed to continue the control struggle, the first by implying the physician is forcing the drug on the patient (this patient will be noncompliant within 12 hours) and the second by provoking argument. The dialogue continues.

Similarly, all the patient's problems can be addressed if the patient wishes: housing, money, vocational training, marital relationship, relationship with mother, early memories of sexual abuse. These may be problems we think the patient has; but he or she may or may not identify them as problems. If the patient does not identify them, then they do not exist as far as relationship management is concerned. If the patient identifies them, they can be addressed within relationship management. It should not be the treatment team's decision that a patient needs to talk about early sexual abuse. However, if the patient wants to talk about it with therapist X, then therapist X should be willing to listen. But therapist X must quell his or her usual curiosity and personal/professional need to explore and uncover to bring about a healing catharsis. Maybe a catharsis will occur. But it must happen under this patient's own direction and control. The therapist is not responsible for it. The larger problem, the manner in which the patient engages in distorted and distorting interpersonal negotiations, must be managed first.

> "I hate my mother."
> "Did you want to talk about your mother?"
> "No. There's no use."
> "OK."

This small piece of dialogue illustrates a rule for dialoguing with a borderline patient. Usually, when a patient mentions something or someone in a manner that suggests it has importance, either by commission or omission, we as trained interviewers "pick up on it." We might say, "You sound pretty angry at your mother" or "You didn't mention your father."

Picking up on it usually entails a direct question, a mirroring response, a reflection, or an empathic summation. Behind all of these responses lies an attempt to have the patient continue talking on this subject. That is what we want, and it is implied in the tone, tenor, and construct of our responses. The borderline patient, working at the process level, will then respond to our covert need or wish to have him or her talk on this subject. It is the direction we want the patient to go. The patient will, as part of the ongoing negotiation with us, in a need to control the definition of the situation, then oppose the very direction he or she was proposing or hinting at.

To manage this process with the borderline patient, the interviewer should always insert a simple question first: "Do you want to talk about it?" And the interviewer should accept whatever the patient answers to this.

## Continuity of Care

One inpatient psychiatrist, having made a diagnosis of borderline personality disorder, immediately discharges the patient, no matter the threat or protestation. At least he does not collude in the usual destructive inpatient iatrogenic processes. But is the patient helped by this abrupt rejection? Some probably are. They take this as a total failure of the uncaring, incompetent psychiatric system, forswear psychiatry once and for all, and get on with their lives. Most probably write off just this one psychiatrist and find themselves a more amenable health care system. This "rejection" is probably better or safer than a protracted messy admission. But absolute boundaries can be applied without rejection, matter of factly. The door is not closed. Cooperation with the development of a long-term relationship and plan is not abrogated.

One of the more important things an inpatient admission can accomplish with a borderline patient is the establishment of a long-term, coordinated care plan. This means conferencing: conferencing with the patient, the family, outpatient therapists, social agencies, clergy, and family doctors and the earlier the better. If at all possible, they should be taught the principles of relationship management. This may require several meetings and lengthy reviews of the patient's behavior and relationship with these others, and all their feelings and fantasies about this patient. In establishing a long-range plan, a good rule of thumb is: Control that which can be controlled, but do not attempt to control that which cannot. If the minister won't come in and doesn't seem to buy relationship management, then consider the minister to be part of the borderline system and interact with him or her in the same manner as prescribed for the patient.

If the patient is repeatedly admitted in crisis and the outpatient therapist cannot or will not institute relationship management, consider terminating the relationship with the outpatient therapist and refusing all admissions. In doing this, we, like the discharging psychiatrist mentioned above, are at least doing no more harm. This can be stated quite boldly to the recalcitrant therapist: "I will not help you harm this patient."

### The Open Bed Gambit

On the other hand, wonderful progress can be made with a cooperative and adaptive outpatient service. If they can adopt relationship management, further crises and admissions can be prevented. In some difficult situations, where the pressure placed on the outpatient therapist by the patient is extreme (high lethality, very public displays), the inpatient and outpatient services can combine forces to manage the relationship. For example, if the pattern has been one in which the patient repeatedly increases the stakes until the outpatient therapist reluctantly hospitalizes the patient and the inpatient service reluctantly accepts him or her, this can be turned around with the following agreement: The patient will always decide when and if hospitalization is necessary. No matter the crisis, the therapist will always ask the patient about wanting to go in or not and always respect the patient's wishes. The patient will always be accepted to a bed on the inpatient service as requested, but once in, the inpatient approach will be exactly as described in this book. This plan can be formulated and contracted in a conference with the outpatient therapist, inpatient staff, and patient present.

On hearing of this kind of approach for the first time, the nurses and therapists will say, "God, she'll be in every week" or "We'll never be able to get rid of him." But the goal (at the process level) of this patient's behavior is not simply to be admitted to the hospital and satisfy dependency needs (this is a common and often wrong formulation), but to continue to engage the outpatient therapist and to reengage the inpatient staff in the distorted negotiations about control and competence, to continue the struggle, the vacillation, the externalization of both sides of the self-system conflict. A simple untroubled admission will not reinforce this. In fact, the patient may test this new contract once but after that not need or request admission.

## STAFF DIFFERENCES

Some *staff* members do better with borderline patients than do others. The staff who don't do well are often vulnerable to process-level distorting negotiations, vulnerable in the sense that they have excessive control needs, or aren't confident about their own goodness, worth, and competence. The borderline patient will sense these vulnerabilities and focus dialogue around them. It is also difficult for trained mental health professionals steeped in psychoanalytic language and perceptions to shift to this model. Borderline patients should be assigned to staff who do well with them. To do otherwise is the equivalent of knowingly giving a patient the wrong medication. Unfortunately, there are mental health workers who do very poorly with borderline patients, contributing to their incompetence and bad behavior, but who feel they do well with them. They seem to need, for their own continuing sense of competence and worth, to "carry" very disturbed and disturbing patients. It is not unheard of for a psychiatrist to carry such a patient for years, seeing the patient many times a week plus phone calls, believing that this is heroic life- and soul-saving activity. Intensive case management may be good for some chronic psychotics; but this intensity applied to a borderline is self-deluding and destructive. Borderline patients should be assigned only to experienced, competent therapists with unconflicted, unambiguous self-systems of their own. We must not use them to satisfy our own grandiose needs. Being a good therapist is not always the same as being a nice therapist.

Wards in conflict should not accept borderline patients. Wards with large numbers of adolescents should think twice before accepting a difficult borderline patient. The acting out, the testing of limits, the ongoing pathological negotiation may become group focused, may multiply in kind and intensity. A ward with an anxious, uncertain, lawsuit phobic psychiatrist should not accept a borderline patient. And, if a ward has had a very recent suicide, it should be cautious about admitting a borderline patient. These and a host of other factors make it very difficult for an inpatient service to apply and honor, in a calm, secure fashion, the social contract necessary to ensure short, constructive admissions of borderline patients.

Mr. S. had been hospitalized, to our knowledge, 45 times in 14 different hospitals since 1974. In fact, he had spent almost his entire adult life in the hospital, with the exception of a few days to a few weeks between each admission. He was diagnosed variously as schizophrenic, schizoaffective, and personality disordered. It was never actually clear to what extent he had ever been actively psychotic. His hospitalizations had begun in his teens. He had seizures, or pseudoseizures, he threatened suicide, he made suicide "attempts," he self-mutilated in minor ways, and he frequently declared himself out of control and helpless. He could also be articulate and, on one occasion, was interviewed by and performed remarkably well for a television program on institutions. He was frequently made involuntary, secluded, and put on one-to-one observation. The staff of the outpatient service that had taken him several times, briefly, and returned him each time and the staff of the inpatient ward asked for a consultation.

The ongoing relationship this man had with the institution and his therapists was analyzed. Relationship management principles were applied. The staff of both services were ready to adopt this approach. This is important. In many circumstances the staff are just not ready to give up their other concepts and activities. For Mr. S. a written contract was devised. (For short admissions, a verbal contract will suffice. For these complex long-standing distortions, a written contract may help both patient and staff.) This contract, with the exception of some gratuitous editorial comments, which have been bracketed, can serve as a model for similar situations.

### AGREEMENT BETWEEN A.S. AND THE PROGRAM

[The goal of this agreement is to foster independence and self-sufficiency by allowing Mr. S. to make decisions and assume control over his own life.]

1. Mr. S. will be maintained as a voluntary patient while on the program.
2. While in the hospital, Mr. S. will reside on the open end of the ward and will have complete privileges.
3. Mr. S. will determine his own program, including discharge plans.
4. Staff may act as resources to Mr. S. by providing him with information if specifically asked to do so, but they will not offer advice or assistance [since Mr. S. is capable of doing things himself.] Likewise, staff will provide no direction to agencies outside the hospital, which will be told to use their own discretion and judgment in dealing with Mr. S.
5. A bed on the ward will be held open for Mr. S. once he returns to the community, and he may access it whenever he wishes.
6. If Mr. S. has a seizure or harms himself in any way, he will be treated medically as needed. No other special procedures will be instituted. Specifically, he will not be certified, placed on one-to-one, or have his privileges curtailed.
7. Should Mr. S. be admitted to the hospital after hours or on a weekend under a certificate, the certificate (involuntary status or committal) will be removed at the earliest opportunity and Mr. S. will resume his usual status as a voluntary patient.

8. Primary contact with Mr. S. will be through his therapist, Mrs. A.; her backup, Mr. B.; and the team leader, Mrs. C. These people should be contacted if there are any questions.

SIGNED: A.S.    SIGNED BY ABOVE TEAM MEMBERS:
DATED:

Shortly after this contract was struck, Mr. S. arranged his own discharge, his own aftercare, and for his own family doctor, and discharged himself and began attending the outpatient clinic. He has remained out of the hospital to this date, approximately 2 years.

# 8

---

# Outpatient Management

Everybody gets in trouble treating borderline patients. More accurately, most borderline patients get in trouble and most of their therapists are, at times, perplexed, puzzled, stressed, and downright troubled. How should we treat them? The range of opinions on this subject stretches from "Don't do it," to supportive therapy, to cognitive therapy, to group therapy, to psychoanalytic therapy with some modifications in the early stages, to a sort of all-purpose mothering in which the client has access to the therapist at all times (Sederer & Thorbeck, 1986; Waldinger, 1987; Gabbard, 1989a; Aronson, 1989; Schaffer, 1990; Stone, 1990a). Each of these opinions is built around formidable theory and some individual successes.

What is written about the therapy of borderline patients may or may not resemble what actually happens. It seems that most therapists working with borderline clients, no matter their theoretical persuasion, get caught up in a cycle of support, encouragement, advice, interpretation, frustration, pills, crisis management, hope, and hopelessness. Many *carry* their borderline clients for years as long-suffering but dedicated therapists ("*My* borderline is driving me crazy"). Others try varieties of psychoanalytic therapy and supportive therapy, repeatedly get in trouble, and eventually learn that less is better. They learn that the less they do for their clients, the more their clients do for themselves. Unfortunately, examples abound where dedicated therapists give of themselves as much as 5 hours a week plus phone calls, get completely caught up in the distorted interpersonal negotiations, and maintain their clients in states of crisis-ridden dependency. "Don't do it" would be good advice for these therapists. The concepts espoused to justify this kind of activity arise from earlier spectrum disorder concepts. For example: "These patients are borderline psychotic, their ego defenses are primitive and weak, they are always in danger of ego fragmentation, years of supportive ego infusion and/or deep reconstructive work are required, and periodic regression is expected."

The therapists who have learned that less is better often still get in trouble in several ways. Their patients communicate to them through third parties, trips to the emergency department and use of more impressive currency, and the therapist is drawn back in. If the therapist is working in a context that doesn't support less is better, a context with anxious administrators and supervisors, or a context of true believers in some other model, it is very difficult for such a therapist to maintain the new outlook. Finally, these therapists make a predictable mistake. They have discovered less is better, they sit quietly, they tell their clients that they don't know and that they have run out of ideas, and they don't offer extra time or new pills. The clients come back next week and report some positive change or action: "I visited my sister" or "I took that new job" or "I feel better." By instinct, by simple social imperative, by training, these therapists respond with support, congratulations, even delight. If not by the end of that session, then predictably by the next session, all will have turned to dust. The therapists have understood that their clients show more competence when not permitted so much dependency, but they have not understood the extent to which their clients' behavior is interlocked, in an oppositional sense, with their own. It is hard to do, but when a borderline client reports some positive change, the therapist must show nothing more than interest.

"I got a job."
"Oh, what kind?"
"With Smith, Baldwin and Ciccerelli."
"As a secretary?"
"Just a file clerk."

It is very difficult to not respond or to respond in a neutral fashion when the client reports some positive change. To get past this social difficulty a paradoxical or mildly contrary response can be used:

> "Are you sure you're up to a full-time job?"
> Or, "That's a pretty demanding position."
> Or, "Doesn't that mean getting up at 5 a.m.?"
> Or even, "That kind of job doesn't pay very well does it?"

The imperative of the borderline dialogue will propel the client to then defend, own, argue for the positive decision. If the therapist supports or cheerleads the client's positive action, the client must assume a contrary position.

> "I got that job as secretary."
> "That's wonderful."
> "But I can't stand the boss, and the other secretaries are already dumping all the crap on me. I'm thinking of quitting."

The therapist can recover by reverting to a neutral or negative stance:

> "Well, I guess the job isn't so wonderful after all."
> "At least it's better than welfare."
> "I dunno. Does it pay much more than welfare?"

## CONTRACT

The contract for outpatient treatment within relationship management is very simple but requires some techniques to present and maintain. "I can see you once a week or once every 2 weeks. I don't know if it will help you or not. I don't have any advice to give you, but if you would like to see me we can get together and talk. I also don't have any suggestions about medication, but we can talk about what may have helped you or not in the past. I'm not available between sessions for either phone calls or extra visits. What do you think?"

Of course, the dialogue will begin immediately. The interpersonal negotiation will begin immediately, and the therapist must then begin the relationship management approach immediately: This client is an intelligent competent adult. You are being honest. You really don't know if the client seeing you will be of help or not. But you will at least do no harm.

This initial dialogue is crucial. If it goes well, the client will be prevented from introducing distortions at the outset, and will, by the end of the interview, have assumed some responsibility, displayed competence, and made the decision regarding treatment.

Now, when a new therapist-to-be approaches a borderline client with this approach firmly in mind, the interview may proceed surprisingly smoothly. The client, it seems, can often read the course of the dialogue from the outset, presumably from the therapist's stance, calm composure, and tone of voice. The client may not test this. At some level the client may in fact be pleased to be treated as a competent adult for once. The contract is easily struck and may not be severely tested until the therapist has an off day.

Another client, however, may immediately attempt to re-create the distorted negotiations:

"Do you think I should come?"
Or, "I want to get off this Valium."
Or, "That won't help me. I need more."
Or, "What do I do when I get suicidal?"
Or, "I took an overdose last night."

At this point it is necessary to utilize the techniques previously outlined: slow the interview down; use silence, short empathic responses, neutral responses; assume contrary positions; use some paradoxical statements. All of these are designed to leave this decision entirely in the hands of the client. For example, as response to the above five client statements:

"I don't know if it will help or not."
"It's very hard to get off drugs like Valium."
"Maybe you do need more than I can offer."
"I don't know. What helps you get past that usually?"

"That reminds me. One of my rules is that if a client of mine abuses the pills I prescribe, and I find out about it, I no longer prescribe any pills for that person."

For alcohol and drug abuse, the rules are simple. "I never see clients who are high or intoxicated. Should you come for an appointment high or intoxicated, you will be asked to leave. If you won't leave, you will be escorted from the building. But your regular appointment will always be available for you the next week. What you do with drugs and alcohol between sessions is entirely up to you."

Of course, in the sessions the possible treatment resources for alcohol and drug problems can be discussed. But any initiative, any movement, any decision to attend an alcohol or drug program such as Alcoholics Anonymous must remain the client's. They usually know more about them than the therapists do anyway. In this manner, a client who undertakes a drug or alcohol rehabilitation program owns and remains responsible for his or her decision, compliance with the program, and abstinence. The client has then taken the first step toward possible rehabilitation.

If the drug abuse problem is excessive use of prescription drugs (acquired somewhere else, because if this client is abusing the therapist's prescribed medication, the therapist will stop prescribing it), reducing and weaning off these drugs is up to the client. The therapist may use contrary and paradoxical techniques, and then, with some skepticism, participate in the reduction and elimination planned by the client: "It's very hard to get off . . . in fact I've seen very few people able to do it. But if this is the schedule of reduction you want to try, OK, I'll follow it with you, but I'm not sure you can do it."

## SUICIDE

Borderline clients do pose a risk. One follow-up study of borderline patients who received long-term residential treatment revealed a risk of death by suicide of 3% over an average of 14 years (McGlashan, 1986). Stone conducted an outcome study of borderline patients admitted to a residential setting (Stone et al., 1987a;

Stone et al., 1987b; Stone, 1989; Stone, 1990). The overall rate of suicide for patients with borderline personality disorder after an average post discharge interval of 16½ years was 8.9% (Stone, 1990). Among a group of borderline patients treated in a general hospital and followed for an average of 15 years, the suicide rate was 8.5% (Paris et al., 1987). Borderline patients with concurrent mood disorder and substance abuse appear to be at increased risk for serious suicide attempts (Fyer et al., 1988) and completed suicides (Stone, 1990b). One of the strongest predictors of completed suicide is a history of suicide attempts (Kullgren, 1988; Paris et al., 1989; Roy, 1982). As Gunderson and Zanarini emphasize, "the risk is real and must be taken seriously" (1987, p. 10).

Equally factual is the information that "a small but significant percentage of patients who commit suicide do so while inpatients" and that another very high risk population is recently discharged psychiatric inpatients (Roy, 1985, p. 233). It could be argued that hospitalizing a borderline client who has spoken of or "attempted" suicide is simply taking someone from a moderate-risk group and placing him or her in a high-risk group.

From a relationship management perspective, responding to the suicide threats or gestures of a borderline patient, especially responding with hospitalization, is reinforcing the legitimacy of suicide threats and gestures as negotiating currency. When this happens, therapy is untenable (the therapist can be emotionally blackmailed), and, the authors believe, the risk of ultimate successful suicide is increased. It is increased because (a) the more often a suicide gesture is made the more likely death by mistake will occur (wrong pills, too many, the expected rescue being thwarted), (b) the client may need to use increasingly dangerous methods to provoke the same response, and (c) before long, countertransference hate sets in (Main, 1957). The therapist may think "I wish she would do it right and get it over with." We are now at a very bad end to a relationship negotiation: The client is helpless, hopeless, not in control, not responsible, and the client's power lies solely in self-destructive potential. The therapist is continuing to profess hope, competence, and control, but in reality is feeling hopeless, incompetent, not in control, and is telegraphing a wish for the client to go away.

Suicide, self-mutilation, and suicide threats and gestures must be disqualified as legitimate currency. This is first done in the opening social contract statement: "I don't want to see you hurt yourself or kill yourself, but whether you do or not has always been up to you, it has always been within your own power and always will be. I have no way of stopping you or preventing your doing it if that's what you really want to do. So really, there's no point in our even talking about it. In our relationship the decision to hurt yourself or not is entirely up to you.

"If you do overdose or cut yourself and end up in emergency, you may or may not get admitted. What happens is up to you. If you do get admitted, I won't come and see you, but your regular appointment with me will be available when you get out."

Important to understand here is our assumption that in the above occurrence the principal other with whom the patient is negotiating remains the therapist. What happens in the hospital, in this sense, is actually not important. If the therapist dismisses this hospitalization as an unimportant event, it is less likely to recur.

If in fact the hospitalization for self-harm or threat occurs on a ward with which the therapist has no ongoing relationship, the therapist need only tell the ward what has been told to the client. If there is a relationship or the ward is using something like relationship management principles, the therapist could attend a conference, but should, at that conference, maintain the same stance: The therapist will not visit the patient in the hospital but will see him or her upon discharge. Also, it is entirely up to the patient and the ward when the patient is discharged.

The client may of course periodically test the contract of "no response to suicide threats or activity." At these times the therapist needs confidence, a supportive work environment, and a repertoire of techniques. These include

1. Repeating and discussing the original contract.
2. Ignoring the event or statement as if it didn't happen. For example, the "accidental" showing of fresh cuts on the arms, the bottle of aspirin falling out of the purse, the statement "I took five Valium last night" can be ignored. The

therapist simply moves on to other topics: "Would you like a coffee?" "What would you like to talk about today?"

3. Remarking on it in a bland, neutral fashion, as if the event has no special implications. For example, "Have you had those cuts looked at?" "Sounds like you were having a really bad day."

4. If necessary, actively disqualifing this currency and then repeating the original contract. For example, the client catches therapist off guard, gets up quickly, heads for door saying she is going to throw herself on the tracks of the subway. The therapist, unable to ignore this, may say (shout), "*Sit down* for a minute. Now, don't you ever again threaten me with suicide as you head out the door. Yes it is, that's what you were doing. Don't do it again. Now, [calmly] as I said before, I wouldn't like to see you kill or hurt yourself, but whether you do or not. . . ." This new dialogue may end as follows:
"So I'll see you the same time next week."
"If I'm still alive."
"Right, if you're still alive."
If suicide, possible suicide, threatened suicide, and worry about suicide are allowed to creep into the interpersonal negotiations between client and therapist, the therapist is rendered impotent. He or she will not be able to prevent distortions.

5. Never asking about suicide ideation. Now this is difficult advice. All our training tells us not only to ask but to ask in detail. Indeed, we should ask any depressed client, and a therapist can be forgiven for asking a new borderline client. But once the diagnosis is certain and the contract struck, the topic should not be raised by the therapist. Asking a borderline client this question within an ongoing relationship brings nothing but trouble. And silence can be used when the client tentatively broaches the subject.

Indeed, if the therapist has, in a confident fashion, stated the contract above and then clearly given the message that suicide threats, hints, and behaviors will not be either legitimate or powerful currency in this relationship, then the client is unlikely to try to use them.

Further situations and techniques include the following:

The client uses the washroom before coming into the office. She sits down and then states that she has just swallowed a bunch of pills. This is a situation in which the therapist's need to remain composed and move slowly is paramount. Relationship management techniques for handling this situation translate as follows:

"What kind of pills did you take?"

"Amitriptyline."

"Well, let's see. Three or four might make you drowsy but won't do any other harm. If they were 25 milligrams, then up to six or seven probably won't harm you. Above that they could make you really sick, and when you get above, say, 20 of them, they could kill you. You know how much you took. What would you like to do? It's up to you. I'll get you over to the emergency if you want." Then the therapist should be silent and wait for a response.

This dialogue does not support the overdose as currency and gives the client the opportunity to decide herself what she wants done. One can expect this to be played out for a few minutes: "You don't care what happens to me."

"I wouldn't like to see you die from an overdose, but only you know if you're in danger."

But very soon this client will decide herself what is to be done, and the therapist will honor that decision.

A similar technique can be used for the phone call with slurred voice and statement of having taken pills. It is important to remember that nothing is lost by first attempting a relationship management dialogue. "Well, you know how many pills you took. What would you like me to do? It's up to you. I could call a relative or friend or send an ambulance if you want." Again it is important to say little, use silence, and remain neutral.

The client may say, "No. I don't want an ambulance."

The therapist will respond with, "OK," and then wait for the client's next move.

If the client states she has taken a big overdose and then hangs up and the therapist feels compelled to act, the damage that is done by this can be undone later as follows: The therapist tells the client that if she, the client, phones, says she's taken an overdose, and hangs up, the therapist must always have an ambulance sent. This will always occur. The therapist is compelled to do this. But the therapist will not come to the emergency department or visit the patient in the hospital, and *nothing will change* in their relationship.

## TELEPHONE CALLS

Crisis telephone calls from the borderline client are counterproductive. They establish distortions, promote dependency. It is more difficult for a therapist to maintain a relationship management stance on the phone.

They can be handled in two ways. It can be a strict rule for the clinic to decline such calls. Clients are told this. They may call other people and services if they wish. Their calls will not be put through. However, this is a very difficult rule for a clinic to maintain. The emergency may be a real emergency; the problem may be medical. But as experienced therapists and those at crisis centers know, these emergencies are often not real emergencies.

> The therapist took a daytime crisis call from his borderline client. She was in her apartment down the street. She was ready to end it all. She had a bottle of Scotch and vial of 100 antidepressants. She'd already taken some of them. She didn't know how many. No, she wouldn't come to the clinic. All right, he would be down to her apartment in a few minutes (please note previous advice about same-sex therapists). The therapist left the office and found his client's apartment. The door was unlocked. She called for him to enter. Indeed, a bottle of pills and a bottle of Scotch did sit on the table beside her. But so did several lit candles. The curtains were closed. The light was dim. The candles glowed romantically on the client who was lounging in a negligee on soft pillows.

The relationship management approach was quickly instituted for this client, who had taken several overdoses and cut her wrists in the past. This behavior ceased, she terminated therapy a year later, and a further year later the therapist met her once again at a case conference. Only this time she was there on a professional basis, as a counselor in a youth service representing a teenage client.

> Another client was an older woman with severe diabetes and manic-depressive illness. She had compromised kidneys and all too easily became toxic on lithium. It was agreed in the contract with her that she could certainly call between sessions for genuine medical emergencies. One day she called, told the receptionist she had a genuine medical emergency. The therapist took the call. "I knew I couldn't get through unless I told them that," she said. "But I was at a women's auxillary meeting at the faculty club this morning and I saw one of your paintings there and I wondered if you'd let me buy it."

The second way to discourage phone calls is to use very strict relationship management techniques during the initial one or two calls. This is difficult when they happen at inopportune times. Just to get off the phone and back on schedule or out of the office, the therapist may find himself or herself giving advice or offering to see the client tomorrow morning—back to distortions.

With the typical phone call, the first thing the client says is usually provocative, if only because it's a non sequitur. The implication is always one of emergency, of impending death or disaster. The therapist on the other end of the phone must do some internal work to keep from responding to this sense of urgency; then should use the same techniques outlined above. Neutral empathy: "Sounds like you're having a really bad day." Silence; saying as little as possible, curtailing the second or third phrase: "Yeah, does sound bad." Assuming contrary positions: "I don't know. I have no idea what you should do." Sticking to the contract: "No, I can't see you till your next appointment, next Tuesday." And waiting for the switch: The switch will come. The client will finally say, "Well, guess I could . . ." And then the therapist will reiterate, "So I'll see you next Tuesday." The therapist will feel under great pressure to support or reassure, to offer something, anything. The therapist must resist this. But saying something like, "I hope it works out for you" is OK.

This phrase connotes human interest and kindness but does not imply control, superiority, or responsibility.

Such a call may end with the patient angrily hanging up. This should be totally ignored by the therapist at their session next Tuesday. The call may also end with a suicide threat, but this has been discussed above.

## LENGTH OF TREATMENT AND TERMINATION

These two issues often do not pose problems within relationship management. The client will at some point decide to see the therapist less often and decide to terminate. A length of time and a termination date can be negotiated at the outset. Or the contract can be, "You decide how long you want to keep coming to see me, and if you would like to come less often. Just let me know."

The ideal length of therapy is unknown. Some borderline clients have done very well in a few months, left therapy, and gotten on with their lives. Others seem to have benefited from 1 to 2 years of therapy within relationship management.

At a point of termination or reduction in frequency of visits, a flurry of attempts by the client to reengage, to return to the beginning distortions, should be expected. These are handled with the same techniques described above. New statements indicating hopelessness and incompetence are ignored. Paradoxical and contrary statements are used: "Are you sure once every 2 weeks is often enough?" "Are you sure you're ready to terminate?" "Well, you may be quite right. Coming here for 6 months may not have helped at all." Above all, the therapist must resist the impulse to defend what he or she has done, and resist sharing and acting on the inevitable anxiety of separating.

Despite the apparent barrenness of the relationship management approach, most clients stick with it for a while. They engage with the therapist. In fact, contrary statements on the part of the therapist ("You're right, seeing me may not do you any good at all") appear to improve attendance. The word "compliance" is not used because it implies directives or orders from a physician or therapist. If the therapist does not reject, the client will attend and negotiate.

Often most others in the client's life—friends, family, and therapists—have given up and rejected the client. This relationship management therapist, if apparently offering very little, if apparently not very knowledgeable, if apparently only interested and not overly concerned, if apparently warm but not willing to teach, rescue, or mother, is at least not angry and rejecting. And the client is beginning to feel more competent.

For clients who have experienced months or years of some traditional form of therapy, with a repetitious pattern of distorted negotiations; with increasing time and frequency, increasing supportive activity on the part of the therapist, increasing incompetence on the part of the client; with threats, self-mutilation, and dyscontrol used as currency, culminating each time in failure and rejection—for clients who have lived through this, the sudden immersion in a managed relationship with a therapist may seem cold water indeed. Relationship management can be adopted gradually but not too slowly. Better it be introduced in a series of sessions in which the main goal is to discuss, change, and renew the social contract. This can start with a review of all in the past that has failed or made matters worse. It will come clear that what has been going on has not been working. The client will probably readily agree with this. The therapist may have more trouble. Often, when mental health workers review a case and note the various approaches that have not seemed to be of help, they end up recommending more of the same. This is rationalized by such phrases as "It wasn't long enough" or "Not enough consistency" but is more likely based on rescue fantasies and an inability to break mental set. If it hasn't been working, stop doing it.

Now, when we stop doing what hasn't been working and institute a relationship management approach, some clients leave and seek out other therapists or health care systems that will oblige and join with them in the ongoing saga of distorted interpersonal negotiations. There is little that can be done about this but wait for another chance. The new relationship will likely break down. The new pills will likely not work. The client will likely be back in the emergency room within weeks or months. There may be a second or third chance; but if there isn't at least *we* are no longer actively contributing to iatrogenic distress and disability.

## NAMING THE PROBLEM

Within counseling services that don't utilize a medical diagnostic system, naming the problem does not pose much difficulty. Clients identify problems that they bring into therapy for discussion. Relationship management can guide the social contract. The activities of counseling are client centered and problem based. Clients are unlikely to pose such questions as, "What have I got?" or "What's my diagnosis?" although they may ask, "What's wrong with me?" The last question can be answered with, "Well, I guess just those things we've been talking about. You have the problems you told me about." The borderline client may be, as mentioned previously, easier to manage and help within this context than within a medical context.

The medical context requires diagnoses and formulations. Now it should be remembered that the strongest medical diagnoses (in the sense of reliable, valid, and useful) are those based on biology and etiology, and the weakest are those based on patterns of social behavior. The diagnosis of personality disorder implies clusters or patterns of something residing in an individual personality, but is actually based on the observation of behavior (or reported observation) within a social context. The philosophical and conceptual difficulties in this have been discussed previously. It should also be noted that though it remains a noble endeavor for investigators to search for patterns and clusters of behavior that can be reliably and validly packaged as syndromes, which in turn *might* be usefully conceptualized as diseases, the term personality disorder is, in most mental health systems, used in less worthy fashion. It is often used pejoratively and/or to mean not really ill, or not deserving of time and attention, or simply bad as opposed to mad (Reiser & Levenson, 1984).

This means that telling clients that they have borderline personality disorder is not in the same order of necessity as telling clients they have schizophrenia or diabetes. It is not as clear, simple, or useful.

But we do use the term personality disorder, and thus it is unethical not to share this with the client. The question is, how can this be done within a relationship management context? How can this be done without presuming to define the client? It can be done by adhering to two principles: remembering the patient is an intelligent and responsible adult and thus being carefully honest, and using the technique of disqualification. So the answer to, "What's my diagnosis?" can be, "Well, the things you've told me about yourself—cutting yourself, feeling empty, being up and down, having some difficult relationships, and not being sure of your own identity—this is a pattern that a fair number of experts are calling borderline personality disorder, although they certainly don't all agree on what it means, or even if it means anything, and they don't agree on how someone with this pattern can be helped. I can give you a book or some papers on it if you want."

A dialogue may ensue in which the therapist may disqualify personal expertise, claiming not to really know if this label fits or is useful, and thus hand it back to the client. It *is* a possible self-definition. The client may accept it or reject it. The therapist will accept the client's decision. When diagnosis is not permitted to become a vehicle for rancorous distorted negotiations, clients usually don't make an issue of it: All right, that may be what the so-called experts say, but they are individuals with their own specific problems.

The therapist may add, "But I guess you'd agree that what we call the problem is not as important as what might help with the problem."

Of course, the client may come back with, "It is important what I'm labeled. I don't want personality disorder on the hospital records."

At which point the therapist can say, "No, you're right. I was wrong. It is important. I have to put something down though, it's a rule. Here, let me show you the choices. You tell me what you think I should put down." Maybe the client will pick "transient situational disturbance" or maybe go back to "borderline personality disorder" or "depression." Our advice is to go with it. More important than these words on paper is the fact that clients are taking responsibility for their own partial self-definition.

A similar negotiation can occur around other forms, such as insurance and welfare applications. Clients can be given information, told all the rules, and then asked how they would like to see the form filled out. In our experience clients fill out these forms when given the opportunity in a responsible and reasonable fashion. Giving this responsibiltiy to the client does not mean the therapist must participate in fraud. Therapists need only overtly and matter of factly state the limits they are prepared to sign their name to.

## HOLIDAYS

It has been said that many analysts and their patients take their holidays at the same time, a rather neat way of avoiding the problem of dependency. If this is true, it would seem to mean that the perceived dependency is really a problem of habit; and that the habit is not so strong in a different context. This may be a universal experience. Getting away often works.

This also speaks to a fundamental fiction driving many relationships between therapists and borderline clients. The clients believe, or come to believe, or to feel, that they cannot survive, cannot carry on, without their weekly or twice weekly hour with the therapist. Therapists collude with this for their own unconscious reasons. The theorists explain this with projective identification, or the manner in which borderline clients merge with and incorporate their therapists (symbolically) into their own ego structures or self-systems. For the therapist to go away for a few weeks leaves the client feeling abandoned, and likely to cry and rage like a 2-year-old. Indeed, many stories are told by therapists of clients taking themselves to the emergency room with cut wrists the day after the therapist leaves (grief) or taking themselves to the emergency room with cut wrists the day before the therapist returns (rage).

With the exception of a therapy relationship in which a regressed client attends a controlling therapist five times a week for years, such dependency is a fiction, albeit a believed fiction that can drive behavior. When this problem is understood from an interpersonal perspective and placed within relationship management, it can be viewed very differently. Clients are capable of surviving for three weeks without the therapist and are equally capable of behaving in a manner that indicates they can't survive. It is all part of the interpersonal negotiations between client and therapist, and these can be distorted or not. To believe intelligent, responsible patients cannot survive 3 or 4 weeks without seeing their therapist is a gross distortion.

Of course it can be a tricky negotiation. To say, "I'm going on holiday for 4 weeks in July. See you on August 5. You'll be fine" will provoke a display of incompetence. Thus a more careful negotiation is in order and may require the cooperation of a colleague. The goal of this negotiation is to have the client not act badly during the holiday and to make an independent decision about substitute services, so that this does not become a distorted negotiation. Thus the therapist should present holidays in this manner: "I'm going on holiday the last 3 weeks in July. Our next appointment after that can be August 5. While I'm away you could see Mary Brown once or twice if you want to. It's up to you. I could set it up, make you appointments, or just talk with her and give you her number to make your own appointment, if you wanted to do that."

In stable situations this may not be necessary. A simple statement of holiday time and next appointment may suffice. In situations where the appointments with a substitute are offered, the client will accept the offer or reject it and the therapist will honor this decision. The client is likely to say, "No. That's OK. I'd just have to start from scratch again." To which the therapist can respond, "OK, if you're sure you don't want her phone number."

## THERAPY

All of the above appear to address the form of therapy, the therapist-client relationship and not the content of therapy. What about the content of therapy? What should the therapist and client discuss? It would be flippant to answer it doesn't matter. But it might be accurate to say we don't know. With borderline clients we do feel managing the relationship is paramount, the real work to be done, and, essentially, the corrective experience. Borderline clients do come with numerous problems. One way of thinking about this is that they have many problems that we would like to be able to help them with but that they also have one big problem that overrides all others. And this is the kind of relationship they attempt to construct with therapists. Until and unless this is managed, none of the other problems can be addressed. Managing the relationship creates a context within which the client, in the company of an empathic and interested other, may address problems.

Early sexual abuse appears to be a common experience for many borderline clients (Ogata et al., 1990; Herman et al., 1989; Bryer et al., 1987). Conventional therapy would have us explore this in depth and then possibly apply or recommend therapy, therapy usually meaning more and more talking, remembering, reliving, catharting, coming to terms with, in this relationship or in a group. All of this can happen in relationship management. It simply must be directed by, driven by the client. We must not try to impose this process. The client may or may not decide to go through it. (See case studies in Chapter 13 for a typical situation and the relationship management interpretation.)

A counselor was having a great deal of difficulty with a client. Every time he found a boarding home for his client, the placement broke down within days. The counselor was running out of options, and ruining his reputation with boarding homes. The consultant was puzzled by this. The counselor felt compelled to solve the client's housing problem for him, and this problem had become the dominant and singular problem being addressed week after week in the counseling sessions. Why had this problem become central? It turned out that the counselor, though offering general case management, was employed by an agency that saw housing as job 1. The counselor believed he wasn't doing his job unless he found housing for the client. It appeared that this issue became central because of the counselor's vulnerability, not the client's. Was this client actually capable of looking through a list of boarding homes and phoning them himself? Yes. Was this client actually capable of visiting these homes and talking with the landladies himself? Yes. So why was the counselor doing this for him and thus letting the choice of a home, placement in that home, and subsequent behavior in that home become currency in their now distorted interpersonal negotiations? Because he felt he was paid to do this.

With consultation the counselor came to understand that his wish to have the client contentedly living with a roof over his head and three square meals a day would more likely come true if he stopped trying to do it *for* his client, and if he simply said to the client, "I've run out of ideas and suggestions. Here's a list of all that's available if you'd like to try yourself. You can use my phone if you want."

In this case example the content, the problem focus, was probably determined by the therapist's assumed role. As with most such problems, it proved to be not substantive, and easily resolved when separated from the ongoing interpersonal negotiations.

One could list many of the ostensible problems brought into therapy by borderline patients: housing, relationships, anger, emotional lability, impulsivity, loneliness, alcohol or drug abuse, sequelae of physical, emotional or sexual abuse, education, employment, training; and even include in this list a number of problems that are defined by psychodynamic formulation, such as post-traumatic stress disorder, dependency or individuation conflicts, and so on. Usually the manner in which a problem is defined is determined by the model or school of therapy inhabited by the therapist. In relationship management the way these problems are defined is left to the client. Also, the way they are addressed is left to the client.

A very intelligent, well-read borderline client in group therapy had anxiety attacks every time the phone rang. She wouldn't answer it, and thus was isolating herself. She also revealed that some years before she had once picked up the phone to be told her mother had died unexpectedly. She might learn any number of terrible things if she answered the phone. This connection between her mother's death and her telephone phobia was as clear to the client as it was to the therapist. And what an obvious target for psychotherapeutic interpretation. The therapist ignored relationship management principles and began a grief-provoking exploration of the mother's death and the client's reaction to the original phone call. The client told the therapist he was way off base, this was not the real problem, and it wouldn't help her get a job or do better with her daughter. In traditional therapies this might be seen as resistance. Within relationship management it is interpreted to mean that the interpersonal negotiations between client and therapist remain paramount, no matter how accurate the interpretation. The client left the group early. At the next group meeting, the therapist reverted to relationship management principles, declared his own uncertainty about what was important. The client then reverted to competence, made insightful interpretations of her own, and stated her own plan for overcoming her problem.

It was felt initially that relationship management should be used in the initial phase of therapy and could then be followed by more traditional forms—analytic, cognitive; and so on. Sometimes this is possible; at least sometimes it is possible, once the relationship is under control, to engage in some of those traditional therapy practices: uncovering, suggesting, interpreting, reframing, directing, supporting. Usually with borderline patients these activities bring about a quick return to a distorted and distorting dialogue. We no longer think it is particularly important to lead the client into a more traditional intrapsychic exploration, and we think that it is often counterproductive. Nothing is lost, however, if the therapist is willing to revert quickly to relationship management, using such phrases as, "I was probably wrong" and "No, you're right. I can't really know what it's like to be in your shoes."

What about the need for deep intrapsychic restructuring? We think this way of viewing human problems is more satisfying to therapists than to clients. Perhaps the notion of psychic structures that need to be explored and rearranged is useful in the treatment of some neurotic clients. It is counterproductive with borderline clients.

All the above might also be criticized as superficial. We are dealing with interpersonal behavior, social behavior, and behavioral change without changing or attempting to change the underlying intrapsychic processes. The key here is the word "underlying." It betrays an assumption that the intrapsychic level of activity and analysis is primary and that the interpersonal is secondary. But there is another way of looking at primacy. In a hierarchy of levels of organization the biological undoubtedly forms the base. Next up the ladder, however, might be the social/interpersonal level of organization, with the intrapsychic taking its place at the (superficial) top. Studies of infants and animals would indicate this is the way things happen. First the biological, then the social, and then, for humans, the intrapsychic. So we make no apologies for not addressing, in relationship management, the intrapsychic level. Changes at the intrapsychic level of organization may simply follow changes in social behavior. Indeed, our clinical experience seems to indicate that while changes in social behavior often lead to apparent or reported changes in intrapsychic phenomena, changes in intrapsychic components seldom, alone, lead to behavioral change. Insight is a highly overrated commodity. Besides, our job as mental health workers is to assist our clients to achieve increased mental health as measured by their activities and reported feelings in the most efficacious manner possible, and not to engage in costly elegant explorations of the vicissitudes of human experience. This can be left to novelists, or, by mutual informed consent, analysts and their analysands.

## COUPLES

Whether or not couple therapy with borderline clients is more effective than individual therapy is not at issue here. Clients may be seen with their spouse if they request it and the spouse agrees, and there are some circumstances in which it is wise for the therapist to declare he or she will see the client only with the spouse. In seeing the couple in the first instance the therapist need only stick to relationship management principles. "I'm willing to see you together, but I don't know if I can do any good or not, it's up to you . . ." Here the therapist needs to resist selling the idea, to resist directing and structuring the session, and resist making systemic interpretations—all the things couple therapists normally do. These are intelligent adults; it is their relationship. Their definitions of what is wrong are as likely to be valid as the therapist's. If the therapist does not stick to relationship management principles, therapy with this kind of couple will quickly lead to the worst kind of distortions. "It is your fault we're fighting, breaking up." "Now he's so angry at me he won't talk."

A husband may turn to a therapist to "fix up his wife." She will probably vacillate between this definition of herself as the problem and him being the problem. They may both put pressure on the therapist to "do something." If the therapist gives in to this, a complex three-way distorted dialogue will ensue. The therapist should use the techniques previously described to avoid this, perhaps with more active use of contrary positions: "I have no idea." "Why do you stay together?" "It doesn't look like you have much going for you." To him, "Judy's been in the hospital about six times. I don't know if it helped or not. What do you think?" Often the husband who has been pushing for some active medical intervention, when handed the responsibility with the therapist declaring he or she doesn't know, will immediately switch to a declaration that nothing medical has helped in the past. Then the therapist can say, "Well, what do the two of you want to do?"

This leads to the concept of a borderline system. There are many situations in which both the client and the spouse regularly communicate with the therapist in apparent crises. The communications may be contradictory, alternately or contiguously. He calls and says she's about to kill herself. She calls and says he's threatening to walk out the door. He calls to say she should be in the hospital. She calls to say he should be in the hospital. What are therapists to do besides pull out their hair and attend their own therapist? It is bad enough dealing with one client trying to impose one kind of distortion; now we have two clients distorting in a triangular fashion.

A useful approach to this is to think of the couple as a single organism, a single organism attempting to establish one distorted relationship pattern with the therapist. This single organism does have two different voices, but the therapist can consider both to be calling and speaking when one is speaking. Thinking this way, the therapist can get away from trying to guess which content, if any, is more accurate. Instead, the therapist can interpret the process interpersonal level as a single organism, the couple, communicating that it (they) is helpless, out of control, incompetent. Now the therapist knows how to respond, and these crises will settle.

In the worst circumstances when it seems impossible to prevent distortions because both parties are so active, it can be wise for the therapist to declare he or she is willing, from this point on, to see them only together, at the same time; and will not talk to either one without the other present.

## DAY HOSPITAL

Day hospitals offer fewer opportunities for iatrogenic distortions than do inpatient services but more than outpatient services. All that has been said about both inpatient management and outpatient management can be applied to day hospital management.

The issue here is really only the participation in programs. If the client is continuing in therapy with one principal other, that is continuing in a managed relationship with a prime therapist, then the individual programs the client might or might not attend need not be run on relationship management principles. Perhaps it would be wise for them to adopt some of these principles, but they need not interact with the client in the manner described here. The client is dialoguing with the therapist. What is important is that the client's attendance at any programs be his or her own choice and responsibility. The therapist doesn't know if they would help or not. Yes, ceramics does sound like a pretty juvenile activity. Yes, it does sound like the group was more disturbing than helpful. I don't know if you should continue or not. Is any of it helpful? It's up to you.

# Part III
## Treatment of
## Related Problems

# 9

## Borderline Behavior in Adolescents

*with*
ROD WACHSMUTH, M.D.*

Many mental health workers who also happen to be the parents of teenagers have been known to proclaim in moments of exasperation that all adolescents are borderline. This may be an extreme judgment, but they are responding to some similarity between the two conditions.

The 16-year-old wanders into the kitchen and says to her mother, "Is it okay if I hitchhike into town tonight with Tracy?"

The mother looks up from what she's doing. "How many times have I told you you're not hitchhiking?"

"I wouldn't do it alone."

"Alone, together, the answer's no."

"Tracy does it all the time."

"Does her mother know?"

"Sure. And she lets her stay out as long as she wants."

"Well, you're not Tracy and I'm not Tracy's mother."

"She trusts her."

"Is that what you call it?"

"You're so horrible."

"Why don't you do some of your homework before supper?"

*Dr. Wachsmuth is Assistant Professor of Psychiatry and Director of the Eating Disorder Program in the Department of Psychiatry at the Hospital for Sick Children, University of Toronto.

The teenager whirls around, heads for the bathroom, shouts over her shoulder, "You always treat me like a baby, you never trust me."

The mother shouts at the closing door, "Of course I trust you, Marcie."

Marcie shouts through the door, "No you don't. You never do."

"Well, how can I, if you want to go hitchhiking and get yourself . . . beat up or something?"

With our own children we might or might not navigate through this dialogue successfully. We will probably get caught up in it. The images of things that could happen are too strong, and our own children know our Achilles' heels: "You don't love me. You don't trust me. All the other parents. . . ."

When the dialogue is occurring with another parent, it is easier to entertain interpretations beyond the content issues. It is difficult for a parent receiving the communication from the child to understand immediately that hitchhiking into town is a fleeting, perhaps ambivalent wish of her daughter's, and that the moment she asked the question of her mother they were into a more important negotiation about some of the changing parameters of their parent-child relationship. "Trust" was the code word used, but the relationship parameters being negotiated probably have more to do with control and responsibility. And, of course, a profoundly adolescent question is being asked: "Do you love me enough to control me?"

The father who sees his daughter only on weekends is driving her back to her mother's. Her brother is in the back seat. After a few minutes of silence the daughter starts muttering and sobbing. "I hate my life. I've got zits, I can't do algebra, I don't have any clothes to wear, I'm always fighting with Mom, Tina's such a bitch siding with Louisa, I hate all my teachers, and that little bugger Jonathan, you know I could just kill him sometimes, I wish I was dead."

The little brother in the back seat has enough sense to keep his mouth shut.

Father is plummeted into depressive guilt-ridden ruminations. Why can't she do her math? Why are she and her mother fighting? If her hair didn't fall all over her face, she wouldn't get so many zits. And statistics about adolescent suicide flash through his head. He begins to ask her about her schoolwork and her friends, but this merely triggers a litany of further despair: Her ankles are fat, her knees hurt, she doesn't have any money.

This time her father has a flash of insight. He takes her hand and squeezes it and says, "I love you, Sweetie, I really do."

She says, "I know. But I wish you and Mom were still together."

For the rest of their trip they talk, although not for the first time, about their relationship, and what happened some years before. When she leaves the car, she's back to her energetic, exuberant, cheerful self. He feels pretty good too. The kid in the back seat has been listening carefully, but all he contributes is the occasional, "Oh, brother."

Process. That's what it is. Adolescents, like borderlines, are always working at the process level of communication. They are always negotiating something, at least with their parents. It is the relationship they are working on, the various parameters of that relationship, and, of course, the way those parameters will reflect upon their sense of self.

The normal adolescent has normal developmental self-system conflicts, about control, power, worth, competence, autonomy, responsibility, and will externalize these into dialogue with the nearest significant other. With luck, most of the dialogue will occur between a good-enough parent and the child and not between the child and teachers, counselors, therapists, doctors, juvenile authorities, probation officers, and police. As with the adult borderline client, there are safe and less safe venues in which the adolescent may externalize conflicts.

Managing a borderline client and parenting an adolescent require some of the same skills. Some of the differences lie in the negotiations over control and responsibility. The adult borderline client is an adult. The adolescent is becoming an adult.

The 17-year-old in a small town had bought himself a car, but it was registered in his father's name for insurance purposes. He was also skipping school, drinking, coming home drunk in the small hours of the morning, and acting surly and disobedient with his parents. His mother was depressed and guilt ridden, his father unable, it seemed, to assert control. The family attended a therapy session.

The boy slouched sullenly in his chair. The mother sat back with tears in her eyes. The father was saying, "I told him he's grounded, but he just drives away. He won't give me the car keys. What more can I do?"

The therapist says, "He's begging you to take charge. He wants you to control him, even though he's fighting you all the way."

The boy looks up, "What the fuck you know what I want?"

The mother says, "What is it you want from us, Brian?"

The therapist keeps his eyes on the father and repeats his message.

The father says, "All right, Brian, let me have the keys."

Brian: "No fucking way. It's my car."

Father: "See. What more can I do? There's nothing else I can do."

Therapist: "Well, you could let him go on drinking and driving and coming home whenever he likes or you could consider that the car's in your name, he lives in your house, you feed and clothe him, he's stolen the keys to your car."

Father: "What, have him arrested?"

Therapist: "Or let him carry on."

Father: "Brian, you give me those keys now or I'll call the police."

Brian (visibly distressed by this turn of events): "It's my car."

Mother: "He did pay for it himself."

Therapist: "Yeah, in some ways he's a good kid. Right now he's screwing up."

Father: "Give me the keys now, Brian."

Brian: "No way, man."

Father: "So what do I do now?"

Therapist: "There's a phone on the desk."

Father: "You want me to call the police now?"

Therapist shrugs, raises his eyebrows.

The father reaches for the phone: "Well, I know some of them down there. I could ask for Bill Walters."

Brian is squirming. There are tears in his eyes.

The father picks up the phone, dials, says, "Could I have Sergeant Walters, please?"

Brian pulls the keys from his pocket and tosses them to his father, "Here, you can have them." He's crying now.

The mother is distressed by her son's distress, but the father's mood has lifted.

The therapist says, "Okay, now we can talk about some other family rules and expectations." He is using his rule of thumb when dealing with families with badly behaved adolescents: First establish parental authority, and then look at feelings and trust and support and understanding.

## DIAGNOSIS

But what of the actual diagnosis of borderline personality disorder in adolescents? Some textbooks of child and adolescent psychiatry focus exclusively on borderline disorders of childhood, while others deal only with those in adolescence (Meijer & Treffers, 1991). It is unclear whether or not they are writing about the same disorder. While at least two researchers have used adult criteria for borderline personality disorder to show that borderline children can be classified using adult criteria (Petti & Law, 1982; Greenman et al., 1986), demonstrating some reliability, there is considerable question about the validity of the term in childhood (Greenman, et al. 1986; Gualtieri et al., 1983). In a survey of child psychiatrists about the use of the diagnosis "borderline," 53% of respondents used the term with children (Bradley, 1981). Robson (1990) writes that problems in the management of borderline children "are similar in some respects to those encountered in treating children with learning dysfunctions" (p. 734). Wenning (1990) views the borderline condition in childhood as "more closely related to the spectrum of affective disorders than to psychotic disorders" (p. 231). And a prospective study of children between the ages of 6 and 10 years diagnosed as borderline concluded that this diagnosis during childhood did not predict borderline disorder in late adolescence or early adulthood (Lofgren et al., 1991). For an articulation of both sides of this issue, the reader is referred to a debate of the statement "Borderline Personality Exists in Children Under Twelve" printed in the *Journal of the American Academy of Child and Adolescent Psychiatry* (Kernberg, 1990; Shapiro, 1990).

This chapter will not address the possibility of a borderline diagnosis in children under 13. The authors feel that applying such a diagnosis to a child is at best premature. But many of the principles of relationship management outlined in previous chapters can be applied to the acting-out[1] and destructive behaviors of adolescents that resemble those of adult borderline patients. McManus and colleagues (1984, p. 451), as cited by Meijer and Treffers, (1991), describe the "delinquent borderline adolescent" as one "who is superficially socially appropriate, though unable to produce any sustained achievement in work or school, is affectively labile, self-mutilative, prone to brief episodes of paranoid ideation and likely to be involved in relationships where dependency needs are great, but denied and where hostility and instability are prominent."

As in the other chapters, in this chapter we address not only those clients (in this case adolescents) who can, strictly speaking, be diagnosed as borderline with current criteria but also those clinical situations in which the process level of communication predominates.

Use of relationship management with the borderline adolescent does not preclude thorough psychiatric assessment. Yet, on the other hand, the very behaviors that might be amenable to relationship management often make thorough, objective assessment difficult.

At the age of 16, a young man took an overdose of antibiotics and was hospitalized in a psychiatric hospital. From this hospital he eloped, was deemed a suicide risk, and thus

---

1. We are using the term "acting out" to refer to those unhelpful behaviors that usually are called acting out in a clinical setting without meaning to imply a specific underlying intrapsychic mechanism.

returned involuntarily. He eloped again. He was given neuroleptic medication. He regressed. He rebelled. He was given more medication. Whatever struggle he was having before with himself and his parents was externalized and dialogued with the staff. He was transferred to a second and then a third hospital because of breakdowns in the relationship between parents and staff and because of the patient's continuing difficult behavior. Diagnosis was uncertain. He was suspected of having schizophrenia, but most time and energy were put into day-to-day management of his increasing repertoire of bad behaviors. At one point during the third hospitalization, he ran from the hospital, down the street toward a high bridge from which he had said he was going to jump. The senior resident on the ward had run after him, and had "got him just in time and brought him back." He was placed in seclusion on 1:1 observation.

## TREATMENT CONSIDERATIONS

### Responsibility

In relationship management of the adult borderline client, the client is always treated as an intelligent, responsible adult. This assignment of responsibility is not warranted with all adolescents. To understand the level of responsibility that young persons have, or should be assigned, for their own actions and decisions, one must consider chronological age, mental age, legal requirements, family involvement, and living arrangements. In most provinces and states, child protective agencies have a legal mandate for the protection of children below the age of 16. A therapist's contract with a 17-year-old living alone would not be the same as one with a 14-year-old living at home with his or her parents. Laws governing the care and protection of children provide some clear guidelines for the assignment of responsibility, while the adolescent's continuing negotiation about responsibility and control with parents, or parental substitutes, makes the issue less clear. Clinicians, like parents, must continually judge how much responsibility they should expect patients to have for their behavior and decisions, and when the parent(s) should be expected to assert responsibility and control. Where the family is intact, this may be easy to adjudicate. Watch what adolescents do rather than what they say.

Adolescents living away from home may be more involved with one or both parents than they have led us to believe. The clinician might negotiate an adult-to-adult contract with such an adolescent only to find that the child's transactions with parent(s) are far more potent determinants of his or her behavior. In fact, the unwary clinician can become merely a vehicle through which an unhealthy parent-child relationship is exercised.

When beginning treatment with an adolescent, one clinician applies this rule of thumb: The early adolescent is in most respects a child. The parents are responsible, and should be in control. The client in mid adolescence may ask to be treated as an adult and may be given such an opportunity. If this client's behavior indicates otherwise, he or she should be reassigned child status. Older adolescents should be given the responsibility of managing and controlling their own behavior, at least within the context of counseling and therapy. (Parents, of course, must respond differentially to the 18-year-old's normal fluctuations in judgment and responsibility.) The less responsible the patient, the more likely family therapy is indicated; the more responsible the patient, the more feasible is individual therapy.

Fifteen-year-old Susan had a history of an eating disorder and frequent episodes of wrist slashing. Her parents were divorced and she was living with her mother. During the past 6 months in therapy, Susan had cut her wrist on three occasions. The mother called Susan's psychiatrist at home each time and demanded that he come to their home to assess her. On each occasion Susan appeared tearful and angry and refused to provide any information. After each episode the psychiatrist suggested meeting with Susan and her mother together, but Susan refused.

In this vignette the child, though being seen in individual therapy as if a responsible adult, is clearly a child. The therapist has become a conduit through which the child and parent are negotiating, badly, some issues of control and responsibility. The next step for this therapist should be to switch to family therapy, redefine the contract, and assume a major goal of supporting and empowering the mother in her role as responsible (and in-control) parent.

If a borderline transaction with the mother develops, the therapist should apply the techniques of relationship management to the relationship with mother as well. This 15-year-old will be most helped if her mother becomes a parent.

The earlier vignette in which the boy was secluded after his run for the bridge continues:

> The psychiatrist increased the boy's medication. He told the ward staff that he was "fed up" dealing with this boy's behavior, and was going to ask for transfer to another unit where there was "more time to deal with this sort of thing."
>
> Prior to the psychiatrist's initiating a transfer, the case was presented to a consultant. The parents were portrayed as hostile, the boy himself as very ill, though the diagnosis was still uncertain.
>
> The consultant asked the senior resident to describe the bridge incident in more detail. The boy was tall, slim, and in good shape. The resident was 37. The resident repeated his story. The consultant asked how he had managed to catch up with the patient. The resident answered that actually he had run out of breath at one point, stopped to catch his breath, and then noticed that the boy, about 75 yards ahead, had also stopped and was waiting for him.

Here was one interaction described in more detail that indicated some kind of interpersonal negotiation was at work rather than a simple wish to die. Staff, however, were divided on this issue. Some viewed his potential for suicide as minimal and merely "attention-seeking" behavior, while others were convinced that he would eventually kill himself.

## Changing the Social Contract

Two lengthy meetings were held, first with the parents alone and then with the boy present. The new consultant psychiatrist presented as honestly uncertain about the value of the pills, about the diagnosis, and about the correct way of interpreting the boy's behavior. The psychiatrist said that medication and seclusion did not seem to be helpful, but it was not clear that anything had been helpful. He acknowledged that there was some risk that the boy might kill himself, but said it was unclear to him what that risk was. As the psychiatrist talked about his concerns, the parents gradually became allies. At first they asked for answers and expressed fear for their son's safety. When they saw that no nostrums, certainties, and untrustworthy assurances were coming from this consultant, they relaxed, abandoned their defensive postures, and began expressing their own opinions. They agreed further excessive protection and treatment would likely do more harm than good. They agreed he couldn't be kept locked up the rest of his life. They agreed the staff should take some chances by giving him more freedom and responsibility. They also agreed to a reduction in his medication. The new approach, with a move toward the social contract of relationship management, was discussed with the patient in the presence of his parents.

There was an agreement reached that involuntary hospitalization had not been helpful to him. He was subsequently changed to voluntary status, with both patient and parents aware of the full implications of this decision. There was an explicit understanding that the boy might elope again, that staff would not send police after him, and that if he did not return within 24 hours he would be discharged.

Following these meetings, this young man appeared angry and discontent on the ward. He talked about eloping and "teaching everyone a lesson." With the currency of his suicide threats devalued by voluntary status, full privileges, and routine observation, he developed several new provocative behaviors, such as kicking a wastebasket across the corridor. But as the staff interacted with him in a calm, neutral manner, without anger or anxiety, and did not rise to his threats and provocations, simply reminding him he was free to leave if he wanted, he gradually began to participate in ward activities. Eventually he had a full weekend at home. On the first occasion he behaved badly and was brought back to the hospital by his parents. Nothing was changed in his relationship management contract with the ward. After five weekend visits, he remained at home. He attended an outpatient clinic, which was advised about the relationship management principles practiced during his hospitalization. For 4 years after this, he has sent a yearly card or letter to the hospital. He is living with one of his friends and works full-time.

The psychiatrist worked actively with both patient and parents to dispel the myth of diagnostic and therapeutic powers he didn't actually have, and to hand control and responsibility back to them. Important questions that didn't have ready answers were posed, and the implications made clear. The patient and his parents were invited to consider their alternatives and to acknowledge what they would do and would not do. The parents could then be clear about their responsibilities and expectations and the responsibilities they assigned to their son.

**The Problem of Abuse**

While systematic studies of the childhood experiences of borderline adolescents are scarce (Esman, 1989; Meijer & Treffers, 1991), the families have been described as conflict ridden (Walsh, 1977) and characterized by severe psychopathology among the parents (Gunderson et al., 1980). Studies of adolescent patients diagnosed with borderline disorder show that a history of both physical and sexual abuse is common (Ludolph et al., 1990; Westen et al., 1990). Recent investigations in clinical populations of adult patients with borderline disorder suggest a strong association with a history of abusive experiences during childhood (Zanarini et al., 1989; Ogata et al., 1990; Herman et al., 1989; Shearer et al., 1990; Bryer et al., 1987; Byrne et al., 1990). Although some studies have found a higher rate of sexual abuse than physical abuse among adult patients with borderline disorder (Byrne et al., 1990; Ogata et al., 1990), other reports describe a similar rate of physical and sexual abuse among these patients (Bryer et al., 1987; Herman et al., 1989). While the question of continuity between borderline disorders in adolescence and those of adulthood remains unanswered, investigators have increasingly focused on the systematic review of childhood experiences in the history of adolescents (Ludolph et al., 1990; Westen et al., 1990).

Thus, therapists are presented with a dilemma. Seeing an adolescent alone might, and often does, undermine the very parental authority and control that could help the adolescent navigate through this difficult developmental period. But empowering the parents, if the parent(s) have been abusive, could be even more destructive.

Frequently, patients will deny abuse when first asked (Sauzier, 1989; Sorensen & Snow, 1991). More often disclosure of abuse occurs much later in the context of a supportive therapeutic relationship and only after effective management of the borderline behavior.

A 15-year-old girl presented to the emergency room accompanied by her two girlfriends. Her friends informed the casualty officer that Shelly had made several scratches on her arm. The physician attended to her abrasions, noted that no sutures were necessary, and requested a psychiatric consultation. The psychiatric resident on call entered the room where Shelly and her friends were talking loudly. The conversation immediately stopped. After a brief period of silence, Shelly stated directly, "I wanted to kill myself, but I thought that I should come to the hospital to be admitted first." The resident suggested to Shelly that they speak separately.

As Shelly's two friends left the room, the resident heard one say to the other, "I thought this was going to be quick. I have to get home soon."

The following dialogue occurred:

"I want to come into this hospital tonight or I'm going to kill myself."

"So let me see if I understand. You want to be admitted tonight? Which ward did you want to be admitted to?"

Shelly hesitates . . . "Well I don't know . . . the ward where people have a rest."

"You want to come into the ward where people can have a rest? Do you mean the psychiatric ward?"

"Well, I don't like to call it that. That's for crazy people. I need to feel better."

"Well, there are several hospitals in the city with psychiatric wards. None of them are just for people your age. Most patients on the ward are between the ages of 40 and 80."

"I don't want to go anywhere else, I want to be admitted here."

"Well, there may not be any beds here, I don't know. I'll have to check."

As the dialogue proceeded, Shelly admitted voluntarily that she didn't want to die but had run away from home because of physical and sexual abuse and needed a place to stay. The psychiatry resident continued to dialogue with Shelly in the above style. As the psychiatry resident resisted taking over decision making for her, Shelly became increasingly competent and clear about her needs. The psychiatry resident explained that there were social workers available who could assist in finding Shelly a safe place to live and that she could then make decisions about what sort of treatment she wanted. With Shelly's full agreement, the psychiatry resident contacted the local protective agency, a representative of which came to the emergency department and met with Shelly. Together they worked out a temporary living arrangement for Shelly where she could continue with school. The social worker initiated an investigation into the family situation.

Some clinicians would argue that the crisis situation is an ideal time for a victim of maltreatment to talk about the experiences. But it is essential for such discussion to remain in the control of the patient. The patient then has an opportunity to gain some control over life situations without resorting to suicide threats and gestures.[2] Shelly was able to articulate that the central issue for her was finding a safe place to live.

Hospitalization may have pitted her against new authority figures in a control struggle and denied her the opportunity to experience her own competent problem solving.

The resident later learned that Shelly moved in with a foster family and successfully finished her year at school. With the social worker, she found a group to attend where she could deal with her experiences of abuse.

A 14-year-old boy in the care of the protective agency was admitted to a psychiatric ward. The agency social worker informed the ward psychiatrist that Bob had a history of severe sexual abuse by multiple perpetrators, including his father. The agency had placed Bob in a number of different foster homes, but he had become physically aggressive and threatened to hurt people on repeated occasions. The social worker said that Bob felt no one understood what he had gone through, and that he frequently demanded more and more one-to-one time with mental health consultants.

Shortly after Bob arrived on the ward, the psychiatrist was called to intervene in a crisis situation. He arrived on the ward to find Bob sitting at a table in one of the recreation rooms, sobbing, being comforted by a staff nurse. There were several overturned chairs in the room and a smashed plate on the floor. The psychiatrist sat down with Bob and the nurse. The nurse volunteered that Bob had settled in nicely on the ward but then came out of his room screaming that he had been experiencing flashbacks of abuse. He had gone to the dining area, thrown some chairs around, and smashed a plate on the floor. Several male nurses and aides had entered the room, and Bob had stopped shouting and began crying. His assigned nurse had sat down to talk with him just before the psychiatrist arrived.

Bob volunteered, "I guess I made a pretty big mess."

2. See Chapters 2 and 4 for some discussion of the child's sense of helplessness and the adolescent or adult's enduring need to assert control of all interpersonal definitional processes to overcome this sense of helplessness and victimization.

"Yeah, there are a few things thrown around the room."

"It's not my fault you know."

Silence on the part of the psychiatrist.

"I can't help it. I was abused when I was younger. I need a chance to talk with someone every day."

The psychiatrist asked Bob if he wanted a regular appointment with a therapist. He nodded yes emphatically. After talking with Bob in a style that enabled him to express his needs while on the ward, the psychiatrist asked Bob if he would like to know the rules on the ward. Bob indicated that he would. The psychiatrist explained that no patient on the ward was allowed to hurt anyone else or any of the property on the ward. The psychiatrist stated in a neutral, calm manner that any further episodes of this nature would result in the police being called and Bob being discharged.

"But it's not my fault, I was sexually abused. My previous doctor told me I'm depressed."

The psychiatrist simply stated that those were the rules of the ward.

The following day Bob complained that his assigned nurse had not spent enough time with him and said that he might get out of control. The staff went about their business, Bob settled down and began participating in some of the group activities. Within 2 weeks Bob was attending school on the ward and had a part-time job within the hospital. There were no further outbursts.

Relationship managment principles, as applied to the above clinical situation, dictate that the here-and-now situation of Bob's outburst, as a manifestation of his relationship to the ward personnel, needed to be addressed, rather than his history of maltreatment. Nevertheless, it was also important to demonstrate to Bob that his concerns about his abusive experiences were being heard and could become the focus of regular therapeutic contact, if that's what he wanted.

## Suicide

Suicidal thinking and behavior are very common features of borderline conditions in adolescents (Friedman et al., 1983; Pfeffer,
1985; Blumenthal, 1990; Pfeffer, 1991; Runeson & Beskow, 1991;
Stone, 1992). Suicidal, parasuicidal, and self-mutilative behavior
can be directly harmful and sometimes lethal. They can also provoke families, therapists, and health-care systems into displays of
impotence, helplessness, rejection, rage, and control. These very
behaviors that are often called "attention seeking" and "cries for
help" may make effective intervention impossible. They can be very
powerful forms of interactional currency that lead the frightened
family or cautious mental health worker to seek others who will take
responsibility for the borderline adolescent, while simultaneously
absolving the adolescent from responsibility. In negotiations about
power, control, and responsibility, suicidal and self-mutilative
behaviors are not helpful modes of communication. Relationship
management principles dictate that self-destructive activity and
threats of self-destructive activity be disavowed as legitimate interactional currency within the therapeutic relationship. The following
vignette illustrates this point:

> The therapist had been seeing Mary, 16, on an outpatient
> basis twice a week for the past 3 months. After Mary had over-
> dosed on Tylenol, the psychiatry resident on call had given her
> a tentative diagnosis of depressive mood disorder and had
> referred her to the therapist for individual psychotherapy and
> consideration of an antidepressant trial. The therapist initially
> had met with Mary and her parents together and told them
> that she would inform them about any issues of safety that
> arose in Mary's therapy, but that otherwise the sessions would
> remain confidential. The parents were extremely anxious and
> asked if they could call the therapist to find out if Mary was sui-
> cidal. The parents had developed a pattern of calling the ther-
> apist weekly to enquire about suicidality.
> Mary talked about her sense of relief following self-
> mutilative acts. She described burning her arms with cigarettes
> and making small incisions in the heels of her feet. The ther-

apist became increasingly anxious about Mary's suicidality and less able to focus on other issues in the sessions. She began to dread the appointment with Mary as well as the phone call from the parents in which she felt obligated to tell them about these behaviors.

The therapist obtained a consultation and was advised to arrange a meeting with Mary and her parents during which she needed to disavow the issue of suicide as legitimate interactional currency. In her meeting with Mary and her parents, the therapist renegotiated their social contract in the following manner:

"Mary, I am concerned about you and I know you have been talking a lot lately about hurting yourself. As you know your parents call each week to see how you are doing in therapy."

Silence from Mary.

"I need to let you and your parents know that it is hard to know how to help you with these behaviors. Whether or not you kill yourself is really your own responsibility. I don't want you to harm yourself, but I have no power to stop you if that is what you really wish to do. Therefore, there is no point in our discussing suicide (self-harm, self-mutilation) in therapy anymore. We'll talk about other things."

Mary sat by silently but listening intently.

The therapist turned to the parents. Mary's father remained silent. Mary's mother became very distraught and said, "Well Doctor, you better be sure this will work. Otherwise my dead daughter will be your responsibility."

The therapist said, "I'm not sure what will work. I cannot guarantee that Mary will not kill herself. I have no easy solutions."

Mary's father turned to the therapist and said, "I understand what you're saying. I can't keep going the way things are right now anyway."

Mary's mother turned to the father and said, "Mary has always been too much trouble for you anyway. You could never take the time for her. I'll get her admitted to the hospital somewhere else."

The therapist responded, "This is really up to the three of

you. I'm telling you what I can do and what I can't do. I don't think the current therapy is working. If you want some other kind of help, that's up to you."

Mary remained silent for a few minutes and then said, "Well, what are we going to talk about if I keep seeing you then?"

The therapist responded, "They are your sessions, Mary, so I guess you need to think about whether there is anything you want to talk about."

The parents continued to argue throughout the session, but the therapist was clear in her message to Mary and her parents. Mary continued in therapy and began to use the sessions to discuss family issues. Although there were long periods of silence in the beginning sessions following the family meeting, the therapist resisted the temptation to suggest a topic for discussion.

In the foregoing vignette, within the relationship between the psychiatrist and Mary, the therapist breaks the spell of immobilization that Mary is weaving with her frequent reference to suicidal thoughts. By making it clear that she cannot do anything about these thoughts, the therapist disavows their interpersonal power. As repeated communication, suicidal thoughts maintain the patient in a needy, helpless position while effectively controlling and limiting the behavior of parents and therapist.

## Hospitalization

Most clinicians would agree that hospitalization of teenagers with acting-out behaviors is to be avoided. At the same time, the hospital is often perceived as a quick solution when a borderline adolescent arrives in the emergency room or places excessive demands on the busy outpatient therapist. Besides, it is a lot to ask any therapist, psychiatrist, or psychiatric resident encountering a new patient to look beyond the presentation of suicidalism or dangerousness to the underlying borderline phenomena in making a decision about admission.

If hospitalization cannot be avoided, length of stay should be as short as possible. While the inpatient milieu has been advocated by others for the containment of acting-out behaviors in the treatment of adult patients with borderline disorder (Kernberg, 1984), no data are available regarding effectiveness of such treatment in the reduction of self-injurious behavior (Winchel & Stanley, 1990). Even less information is available about the effectiveness of the inpatient setting in treatment of adolescents with self-injurious behaviors. The case of the adolescent boy and three psychiatric hospitals, actually spanning 18 months, provides an illustration of how hospitalization was not effective, prolonged the problem, and could have been quite destructive.

If the admission is protracted, discharge may become increasingly difficult. The borderline adolescent patient is especially vulnerable to imposed self-definitions and self-concepts. Psychiatric hospitalization may provide a new identity, partial or all encompassing, with an interesting set of societal expectations and a new repertoire of negotiating behaviors.

Once the patient is admitted, certain principles can assist the clinician in effective management. As in all other interactions with borderline adolescents, the theme of responsibility is central to inpatient management. However, a distinction must be made between the adolescent living outside the family and the adolescent who remains a member of a family. Hospitalization under the former condition puts the psychiatrist and the unit staff in a quasi-parental position, which compromises effective therapeutic work. Hospitalization of a borderline adolescent still living at home can be managed with more success if a working relationship with the parents is sustained.

Monica, 15, lived with her mother and her stepfather and had irregular contact with her biological father who resided in another province with his new wife. Outpatient efforts to treat the disturbed relationship between mother and daughter were made difficult by Monica's repeated suicide gestures. As the outpatient therapist tried to probe the meaning of these self-destructive acts, Monica began to describe dreams in which a large menacing figure loomed before her at her bed when she was a little girl. In these dreams, Monica was attacked and suffocated. As she described these dreams in greater detail, her suicidal behaviors increased in frequency and lethality. During the outpatient sessions, Monica talked about her belief that this reflected the actual behavior of her biological father when she was a preschooler. The mother could not confirm or refute Monica's allegations.

The outpatient therapist became increasingly unsure about how to proceed, and Monica was consequently hospitalized. In hospital, Monica's self-destructive comments and threats were disavowed. Nothing was altered when she raised the issue of hurting herself. Instead, Monica was given the opportunity to participate in ward activities with the other adolescents. She began to show interest in developing relationships with peers. As Monica focused on these activities, she acknowledged to staff that her dreams did not necessarily represent interactions with her biological father. She raised this issue in family meetings. The conflict between mother and daughter increasingly resembled normal parent-adolescent struggles over issues of autonomy. The mother began to give clear signals to Monica about her behavior. Monica eventually indicated her interest in developing a relationship with her biological father. At her request, the father was invited to attend a session. With the mother's agreement, Monica was discharged and visited with her biological father. At follow-up 6 months later, Monica was again living with her mother. They were getting along well and Monica was having significant social success with her peers.

Hospitalization has many pitfalls. The adolescent may learn to use hospitalization as a means of controlling parents, and parents may learn to use the hospital as a means of abrogating their own authority and responsibility. Parental responsibility is then passed from parent to institution and, given the social imperatives and policies of institutions, this responsibility may often be inappropriately accepted. However, given that admissions are often arranged by clinicians who are not the ones who conduct the treatment, the inpatient treatment team requires strategies for dealing with such situations. It is of paramount importance that the inpatient team continue to be frank and vocal in describing what it can and cannot do for the patient and the family. Such communication tends to challenge the image of unconditionality that is often set up around responsibility assumed by the hospital in a crisis admission.

Clinicians frequently find it difficult to maintain a neutral, nondirective position with adult patients. It becomes even more tempting to take on a caretaking posture with adolescents ("I care about you and will assume some responsibility for your welfare"), especially when the family presents to the physician pleading for assistance ("Please doctor. We'll do anything. We just don't want Nancy to die."). By assuming an excessive caretaking posture, the clinician inadvertently accepts responsiblity for the young person's (and family's) behavior. As in work with adult patients, it is important to keep personal needs (e.g., to be seen as smart, competent, loving) in check. This becomes particularly difficult when another professional is insisting on a course of management with which the clinician disagrees.

> The psychiatrist received a message to call a local pediatrician immediately. The pediatrician had been seeing Jody for individual counseling sessions over the past 2 months. Jody had broken up with her boyfriend 3 months ago but had the expectation that they would get back together. She had demanded that her parents give her two hundred dollars to buy a new wardrobe to try and win her boyfriend back. After learning that he was seeing someone else, Jody threatened to take an overdose.
>
> The psychiatrist sensed the pediatrician's distress and volunteered that he could provide a consultation that day. The pediatrician declined the consult and demanded that Jody be admitted to hospital immediately. He stated that he couldn't run the risk that something might happen in the meantime. The psychiatrist attempted to explain the possible consequences of prematurely hospitalizing an adolescent. The pediatrician became further annoyed and said that he would personally arrange her admission elsewhere.
>
> Several days later, the psychiatrist asked the pediatrician about the disposition of the patient. The pediatrician looked rather downcast and said that Jody had been admitted to a pediatric ward in another hospital. The nursing staff were up

in arms because she was frequently on the phone and racing up and down the halls. The pediatrician stated that every time he tried to discharge her she threatened suicide.

In any encounter with an adolescent with borderline features, one must have some sense of the institutional support before defining a social contract that involves issues of safety. For example, in the relationship management of adult patients who become hospitalized, an effective method of disavowing destructive activity is to inform the patient that any such activity will result in immediate discharge. It is essential that the clinician have the support to follow through. Indeed, not to follow through becomes detrimental for the patient who comes to believe that the clinician has been uttering hollow threats or was being dishonest, both of which are rejecting communications. In comparison with an adult, it is often much more difficult to follow through with the discharge of an adolescent from inpatient or outpatient care after destructive activity. If an adolescent is making repeated self-mutilative acts while on an inpatient unit, but discharge is not an option, the alternate response described in previous chapters can be used: Nothing will happen, nothing will change. This is not easy to achieve. All staff must accept this approach as credible, often by first reviewing the fact that the other approaches have not altered behavior, and they must accept that the new stance will be tested.

In summary, it can be easily stated, though application can be very difficult, complex, and frustrating, that management of the borderline adolescent, as inpatient or outpatient, often differs from that of the borderline adult in two fundamental ways: (1) the adolescent may need to be rescued from an abusive situation; and (2) the adolescent's parent(s) may be the party who should be assigned responsibility and control. And while long-term studies of borderline adolescents up to adulthood have not been conducted systematically (Meijer & Treffers, 1991), the clinician has an opportunity to intervene in a way that might prevent chronic pathological interactions with the health care system.

# 10

---

# Borderline Phenomena
# and Personality Disorder

Some years ago one community psychiatry clinic outlawed the use of the diagnostic category "personality disorder." Instead these were said to be people who had problems (relationship, marriage, housing, employment, and so on), did not suffer from something that could be usefully called an illness, and were difficult to help because they habitually behaved in difficult ways in all relationships. It was a noble effort. Unfortunately, the universal need to name everything was stronger than the philosophical position of the clinic director. Other names developed, such as the angry young man syndrome, as in, "What we have here is another angry young man." Perhaps this is better than personality disorder with passive aggressive and sociopathic features. It must be better than "She's married to a psychopath."

The term personality disorder is used pejoratively, not in the literature and not in the classification manuals, but in the day-to-day language of clinics and hospitals. It more often connotes an emotional reaction to the behavior of a given client than a considered diagnostic statement. And this is important to acknowledge. It may prove useful in the future to categorize and subcategorize people with personality disorder, and look for differences in their genetic and developmental makeup, but for the moment what we are really talking about are people who consistently engage in troublesome behavior within interpersonal relationships, including relationships with therapists, counselors, and doctors.

Thus with most, if not all, people we call personality disordered, it may be useful to apply a purely interactional level of analysis, and the interviewing techniques so effective with borderlines. These techniques may not bring about a cure, but they will manage the relationship and decrease inadvertent collusion with destructive patterns of behavior.

The angry young man had been unemployed for 5 years. Numerous counseling and vocational rehabilitation agencies had failed to get him back on track. In frustration they considered offering him a permanent disability pension on medical grounds. This required referral to the psychiatric clinic.

In the first interview with the psychiatrist, the young man's agenda was clear. He was sullen, angry, demanding. What could the psychiatrist do for him? There weren't any decent jobs out there, vocational rehabilitation wasn't worth shit, he could make more money on welfare than washing dishes. What was the doctor going to do for him?

Now it would have been possible to make an elegant formulation about this man's sense of an external locus of control, his entitled demanding, his use of projection, his passive aggressive personality, his excessive dependency needs and denial thereof. But it takes two to interact. The script clearly called for the psychiatrist to try to help him, especially help to convince him he should get a job, and for the psychiatrist to fail miserably. So instead the psychiatrist said, "You're right. If I were you, I'd stay on welfare. It's a hell of a lot better than four bucks an hour washing dishes. You could make more money than that at Stelco, but they're really dirty jobs and you'd never move up."

The angry young man developed a funny look on his face. Was he being had? You could see the struggle going on in his head. To oppose this therapist meant arguing against welfare and for employment. His need to oppose and defeat the psychiatrist won. Being on pogey is lousy. Working is better, he said.

"I don't see that," said the psychiatrist. "There's no shame in it, and most jobs you could get would be lousy. I mean, I got a good job sitting behind this desk, but you're not gonna get my job. Between some minimum wage job and pogey I'd take pogey any time. Besides, there's a recession going on, and there isn't much work anyway."

He could get a job paying 10 bucks an hour, the patient boasted.

Naw, they'd never give it to you. You've got no work history. Stay on welfare.

He hated welfare, man. Any work was better.

Can't see it ever happening, said the psychiatrist.

Christ, he could go down tomorrow and get a job.

That'd be stupid to do. I'd stay on welfare.

And so it went, the psychiatrist arguing pessimistically against gainful employment and for welfare, and the client arguing more and more vociferously for work. Every now and again the client paused, as if he had just heard himself and couldn't believe his ears, but his imperative to defeat the psychiatrist was much greater than any other consideration, and so, despite his other self, he persisted. The only way he could prove the psychiatrist wrong was to get a job—which he did. Unfortunately, there is no long-term follow-up on this case.

Another angry young man wanted help, demanded help, wanted to feel better. He was sullen, provocative. What were we going to do for him?

"Probably nothing," said the psychiatrist.

"Whad'ya mean nothing?"

"As far as I can see, you're a loser. It'd be a waste of my time."

"What right you got to call me a loser?"

"It's not me. You figure you're a loser. You've even got it tattooed on your knuckles." Which indeed he did, LOSER, from thumb to little finger.

"Yeah, but you can help me, right?"

"Probably not. Not as long as you figure you're a loser. Christ, you're on welfare, no girlfriends, no money, drinking and using drugs, probation for B and E. You'll be dead in two to five. *Loser* tattooed on your hand."

"I'm not a loser."

"It's written right there on your knuckles."

"Yeah, but you gotta help me."

"Tell you what. I got nothing to offer you. I don't think I can help. I still think you'll be dead or in jail in two to five. But you get rid of that tattoo on your knuckles and you get a job, I'd be willing to see you again to talk. But I don't think you've got a chance in hell."

The angry young man left, not happily.

A few days later the psychiatrist got a phone call from a plastic surgeon. "Look, I've got this young man in my office, says he's seeing you and has to get this tattoo taken off his fingers."

The surgeon was quite understanding and obliterated the letters spelling LOSER. A few more days passed, and the young man phoned to make a second appointment. He had a janitorial job.

He did not become a model citizen, but these two cases illustrate the interactional imperative. The script they are playing out requires two actors. Unfortunately, professional helpers usually act out their prescribed role of hopeful, encouraging, positive assistance, making it possible for the personality-disordered person to continue to feel justified and powerful through failure. "Even the doctor couldn't get me to stop drinking. How can I be expected to do it. He's educated, makes good money, and he can't do it."

The interpersonal dynamic usually being negotiated by alcoholics and addicts is that of responsibility. Who's responsible for this behavior? Who's responsible for my unhappiness, for my mess? Successful addiction and alcohol agencies understand this. "You're an alcoholic. If you keep drinking, this is what will happen to you. We can offer you some help, but it's up to you. It's up to you whether you keep drinking or not."

Physicians, applying the social contract of the medical model, don't often do well with alcoholics. In fact, they often compound the problem by adding dependency on prescription drugs.

Some of the same techniques used with borderlines can be used with alcoholics, especially the assumption of a contrary position. The alcoholic is asking the therapist for help, advice, asking the therapist to assume some responsibility for the client's drinking.

The contrary position for the therapist is to disavow expertise and avoid responsibility for the client's behavior.

"You know the alcohol services and agencies available better than I do. Have you been to the clinic at Chedoke?"

"Yeah, three times."

"See, you probably know more about them than I do, if they're any good or not. You decide whether you want to go to any of them, and I'll make a referral."

"Stupid bastards want you sober for a month before they take you in."

"Doesn't sound very helpful."

"If I could stay sober for a month, I wouldn't need them."

"Well, it's up to you, I guess."

# 11

## Borderline Phenomena in Schizophrenia

She had spent 18 months in the first hospital, often in difficulty. She was big, had a loud voice, and was easily upset. The hospital never seemed to find the right dose of neuroleptic medication, the right programs, and the right discharge plan. It was too much or too little, they didn't help, she couldn't cope. She was transferred to a second hospital. The team at this hospital was at first puzzled by her long stay in the first hospital because her psychosis appeared to be controlled and she was really, in a gruff way, quite likable. The real problem came to light quickly. Whatever medication the psychiatrist prescribed became a contentious issue within hours. It was too much or too little or the wrong kind. Whatever the nurses asked her to do was unhelpful, not something she liked, too simple or too difficult.

This woman's primary diagnosis was schizophrenia, but her problematic behavior was better understood as a distorted ongoing interpersonal negotiation, or a borderline phenomenon. The issues being transacted were competence and control. The psychiatrist quickly switched to a position of not knowing what was best for this client and gave her control of all facets of her treatment. She was at first taken aback. "You gotta be kidding," she said, trying to give control back to the doctor. He remained steadfast. She made tentative decisions about her own medication, but by the next day was saying the pills weren't working and would the doctor please raise, lower, or change them. He handed these choices back to her. Over the next few days she caught on, began making her own decisions, appeared anxious but delighted with her new-found competence. Very soon she made her own discharge plans, visited and chose a boarding home, and moved on to outpatient care.

When people with schizophrenia exhibit patterns of behavior that are difficult to manage, and these behaviors do not appear to be symptoms or direct consequences of psychosis, they are often thought to have a secondary diagnosis of personality disorder. That is, these are clients with both personality disorder and schizophrenia. Another way of conceptualizing these same behaviors is to think of them as indirect sequelae of schizophrenia, as learned, simplified, or archetypal interactional patterns. The person with schizophrenia has difficulty changing roles, adapting to complex subtle social interactions and expectations, and may adopt a simple, stereotypical behavioral pattern in order to maintain transactional predictability. It is quite common for a client with schizophrenia, especially a young male, to assume a generic oppositional stance in the face of a rather intimidating, controlling, perhaps demeaning health care system. A control struggle ensues.

For practical purposes it is not important which interpretation is most accurate. But it is often useful to consider these troublesome behaviors from an interactional level of analysis, as interpersonal negotiations. Once the problem has been conceptualized in this way, all the techniques described in previous chapters can be used.

Of course, if the behavior in question is driven by delusions or hallucinations or cognitive deficits or even simply very rigid patterns of thought, it will not yield to the techniques for treating borderlines. In fact, the interviewing techniques of silence and assuming contrary positions will likely disturb a psychotic patient. So caution is in order.

But even some behaviors driven by delusion contain interpersonal elements, or another way of saying this is that when the delusion is being expressed in a social context, that context will influence the behavior.

The young woman was convinced that her ex-boyfriend was harrassing her over the radio, through the television, and in the newspaper. She was diligently taking her neuroleptic medication while living in an apartment, and was otherwise symptom free. The ex-boyfriend continued to harrass her. She reported this to her therapist weekly, and weekly he attempted to reassure her and otherwise convince her of her misinterpretation. On the fifth week of this particular symptom, the therapist switched tactics. Instead of reassuring her, he said, "You're right. He is harrassing you and this is really terrible. In fact, it's not only distressing, it's illegal. We'll have to report him to the police. Do you know where he lives now?"

"No."

"OK, we'll first look through the phone book and see if we can find his address and turn him over to the police."

The therapist got out the phone book and engaged in the search, asking for a middle initial, and might he have an unlisted number, and so forth. The patient's interest flagged. She appeared distracted, increasingly distressed, and reluctant to pursue this line of enquiry. Finally, she began to cry and talk of how lonely she felt. The phone book was put away. The young woman never again mentioned the problem of harrassment by the ex-boyfriend, and went on to take courses and get a job.

Now there are several ways of interpreting this minor success. But it seems apparent that the idea of the ex-boyfriend communicating to her through radio, TV, and newspaper remained a reality to her during the sessions in which the therapist attempted to convince her otherwise, and that at least the importance of this idea faded once the therapist not only acknowledged it but pursued it. This woman was not stupid. Though she had schizophrenia and was experiencing direct communication through radio and television, she must have harbored some doubts about her perceptions. Thus perhaps she came to the sessions with a question about whether this was real or not, and when the therapist argued against her perceptions, she was compelled to defend them. This may have helped maintain the idea of reference. When the therapist assumed a contrary posture and she no longer had to defend her perceptions, her doubts poured forth.

The young man was very ill, and staff on the inpatient unit were watching him closely. Neuroleptic medication seemed only to blunt his affect. He remained delusional, and continued to insist on reading the Bible for hours on end and punish himself through prostration and prayer. The staff continued to try to persuade him otherwise, to distract him, and engage him in other activities. This became the focus of their interactions. A consultant was called upon. In the interview with the young man with the other staff present, the consultant agreed with him: Self-abasement, punishment, self-flagellation as a means of becoming worthy of God's consideration had a long history. Perhaps it was a good way to deal with sin and become worthy in the eyes of God. The consultant agreed he should continue praying on his knees and reading the Bible. How much time per day did he feel he should devote to this? Some times were discussed and agreed upon. Was he sure this would be long enough? Yes. The time negotiated was an hour in the morning and an hour in the evening.

By no means did this bring about a cure or even an improvement in the young man's actual psychosis. But his prayers and Bible reading were no longer a contentious issue, he didn't need to do it as much (now that no one was opposing it), and he had time for other things.

This little man had resided in the hospital for 15 years, and it had been many years since anyone had tried community placement. A new energetic rehabilitation team reviewed his case and decided to try. A great deal of work was done with this patient preparing him, finding the right setting, and organizing some fail-safe aftercare in the community. The team would continue following him on a daily basis, and a bed was available should readmission become necessary. Despite all this caution, the family of the patient opposed his placement in the community. A letter was sent to the administrator signed by 11 family members. The administrator handed the letter to the medical director. The medical director supported the team in its endeavors. The family hired a lawyer, and the lawyer phoned the medical director. The lawyer expressed the family's concerns. The medical director reassured the lawyer that all reasonable care and precaution were being used. The lawyer persisted. Despite the medical director's outlining the thought and care that had gone into the plan, the lawyer persisted in voicing concerns of an "I understand, but . . ." variety. Finally, after perhaps half an hour on the phone, the medical director said, "Tell you what we're really going to do. We're going to put a suitcase in his hand tomorrow and drop him off on the highway."

The lawyer immediately became reasonable. She understood the patient wanted to try life in the community. She understood we were doing our very best to make it succeed. In fact, she would go back and do her best to convince the family members that the patient should be given a chance.

And he was. He now lives in the community and calls himself, in his own words, "a new man."

This paradox was used on the lawyer rather than the patient. Perhaps it's an ideal technique to use on someone entering into a negotiation with a trained adversarial advocate. We look forward to the opportunity for further clinical trials.

Another chronic patient was brought forward by the new rehabilitation team. This man was known to perform much better at recreation and sports activities than on the ward, where he assumed a sullen, passive, resistive stance. The problem was he didn't have an opinion about anything. When asked about the possibility of living in a boarding home, he deferred to the opinions of his mother, his psychiatrist, and the nurses. They didn't think he was ready. He was still too sick. At least these were the opinions he told the team. When the team worked with the psychiatrist and the mother, the patient still managed to refer to their doubts and negative opinions. It was decided to use the medical director's authority.

The medical director discovered the patient held no views of his own but used the opinions of others to argue always in the negative. This included activities, clothing, health, illness, and discharge plans. He was immobilized. The medical director had a painting hanging on the wall. He asked the patient, with a smile, what he thought of it. Did he like it? The patient hesitated for a moment. The medical director insisted he wanted to know. The patient said, "I don't like it. It's not very good."

The medical director laughed, the patient smiled shyly, perhaps slyly. What about the one on the other wall? No, he didn't like that one either.

Well, it's not a big point, but some kind of understanding was struck that day, and the medical director and team proceeded with a combination of forced choices and paradoxes, so that in thwarting the staff this man took charge of his own community placement. He now resides happily in a good boarding home and has no intention of ever coming back.

The big man was enraged at being held in the hospital involuntarily. He refused to talk with his psychiatrist. He applied to the review board to overturn his involuntary status. On the basis primarily of his mother's testimony, the review board upheld his involuntary status. He was still enraged, contacted a lawyer, and threatened lawsuits for wrongful confinement. He refused to cooperate with anything or anyone. He was psychotic. Should we try to force treatment on the mother's consent? With adequate neuroleptic medication would his angry oppositional stance evaporate? It was decided the forcing of medication would set the stage for continuing oppositional behavior. This was a chronic illness; a long term perspective had to be considered. So the psychiatrist took the opposite tack. She told the patient he was now voluntary. He could leave if he wanted to. She would like him to stay, but it was now his choice. It was also his choice to take medication or not. He blustered at first, still wanting to fight, but when the new position of the hospital was reiterated he grew quiet, then frightened and anxious, and finally asked if he could stay. He became a voluntary, compliant, and insightful patient.

# 12

## Cautionary Tales

One of the authors was asked to consult on a man who had a "severe personality disorder," who had not lived up to the contract he had agreed upon with staff, and who "should be discharged." The overt reason for the request for consultation was to establish support for the attending psychiatrist's and team's decision to discharge.

The man's behavior was irritating. He lay in bed most of the day. He was obsequious in his verbal responses to nurses, and yet "passive-aggressive" in his actions. He promised to take the antidepressant pills offered, and then spat them out. He also spat on the floor beside his bed, and picked his nose bloody and smeared this on his pillow. Whenever anyone talked to him beyond superficial greetings, he would start to belch. He would agree to most suggestions, such as getting dressed and going to the cafeteria for lunch, but he would follow through only once. Perhaps he was depressed, but mostly he appeared, to those who worked with him, miserable, spiteful, controlling in his passivity and irritating habits.

The consultant was assured by staff that this was how the man usually was, that he had always been rather inadequate and irritating. This was despite a phone call from a niece who claimed that her uncle was rather charming and of high spirits at his best.

The consultant met with the patient on a few occasions, and experienced firsthand his belching, his promises, his brief compliance followed by withdrawal and apathy. The consultant then used each of the techniques described in Chapter 6 to elicit the switch. Through each it was not clear to the consultant whether the dominant experience driving the patient's behavior was the immediate transactional negotiation or something else, something residing in the patient alone. In his final paradoxical maneuver, the consultant took the patient to the outside of the front door of the hospital on a winter day and said, "I give up, it's hopeless, I guess you're hopeless, I agree, you might as well take off now and die in a snowbank."

With no increase in energy, with no interactional spark, with no provoked denial or opposition, with no sense (to the consultant) that he was testing the consultant's resolve, the patient said, "OK," and began to walk away.

"All right, all right," said the consultant. "Come on back. We're going to talk about ECT."

A number of electrical convulsive treatments later, the patient was a very different person, still obsequious, yet not spitting, not belching, up and about, dressed, smiling cautiously, saying he felt much better and was planning his discharge. Of course, in hindsight, it is clear that he had a mood disorder that had not been treated adequately.

This case example illustrates a first caution: labeling people personality disordered because they exhibit behaviors we don't like, and then justifying rejection of them. This can happen and undoubtedly does happen without the existence of the model espoused in this book. But the model may inadvertently give support to discharging, undertreating, not serving some patients who should not be discharged and who should be treated more vigorously. There was probably enough evidence in this man's presentation and past to warrant the diagnosis of refractory depression if the team had not been so angry with him. And the borderline techniques applied to him did not engender the switch. What does this latter idea mean?

The model works when the behavior at hand is truly driven by interpersonal negotiations and not by psychosis, a primary affective state, or cognitive impairment. When these latter factors predominate, the relationship management model should be used only to facilitate other treatment.

Some methods of distinguishing these two situations are outlined in Chapter 6. The behavior alone is not enough. It can be simple and benign (a coy smile, a missed appointment) or it can be dramatic and life threatening (a slashed abdomen, an overdose). Any of these may be driven primarily by immediate interpersonal negotiations or by private factors.

One can come at this differential diagnostic question from either side: Treat thoroughly and vigorously as if the behavior is driven by intrapsychic or brain factors, and when this fails, consider the interpersonal side, or apply the techniques outlined and test the theory of interpersonally driven negotiations first.

Using shorthand, one of the authors might say about a new patient, "I agree, her behavior fits the usual criteria for BPD, but when I interview her she doesn't *play.*" In saying this he is trying to say that he doesn't feel, when talking with and interviewing this client, that her behavior or her statements are dependent on his presence (context bound); that he feels that at least his presence and his negotiations are not the dominant force to which she is responding. Something else is going on. She is being driven, mostly, by her own internal thought processes, her mood, her own cognitive deficits, or even autonomous brain patterns.

Another patient's current behavior and past history from her teens through her twenties into her thirties indicated a borderline personality disorder. She wasn't psychotic, though the possibility of depression was often raised. Through this period of her life, she abused drugs and alcohol and perhaps sustained minor head injuries. When the consultant interviewed her, she didn't "play," she didn't negotiate; his use of neutrality, contrary statements, and paradoxes did not draw from her any kind of rejoinder, and certainly did not provoke a switch. His verbal report to the consultee was that this patient might be borderline, that her behavior appeared borderline, but something else was going on. The relationship management model could be tried to manage some of her behavior, but she could not be discharged, and the option of doing nothing as response to her bad behavior wouldn't work in this case. Interpersonal negotiations were not driving her difficult and self-destructive behavior. Something else was, or it had become a pattern that was now autonomous.

Months later, after a long and difficult period in the hospital, she began responding, began behaving, looking, and interacting better. It may have been the valproic acid she was now receiving, and it may have been a partial seizure problem of some sort. It was clear that to use the relationship management model would have failed and been dangerous.

In using words such as "play," "negotiate," and "currency," this model can be wrongly interpreted to imply that the client's behavior under consideration is conscious, or that at least the client's intent and motivation are conscious. It is then a simple step to the words "manipulation" and "willful"—or even to that rather generic term now being invoked on wards to describe that which is not illness driven—"behavior," as in, "It's not psychosis, it's behavior."

The model is not meant to imply this. The question of conscious versus unconscious is bypassed by this interpersonal model. It is understood that the patient, like the rest of us, is conscious to varying degrees, of the various possible intentions and motivations governing behavior, but that this has little to do with the interpersonal imperative driving it. The patient is to be held responsible but not blamed or punished. Considering these patients responsible for their behavior is not a way of forcing them to acknowledge any nefarious motivations they might have had, but simply the application of an interpersonal and social contract that will shape their behavior in other directions.

In this model conscious versus unconscious is a nonstarter. It is an overburdened distinction at the best of times. In William Styron's description of his depression and suicidal state in *Darkness Visible: A Memoir of Madness*, he looks back on the "theatrical quality about all this . . . I couldn't shake off a sense of melodrama—a melodrama in which I, the victim-to-be of self-murder, was both the solitary actor and lone member of the audience" (Styron, 1990, p. 64). Of course, he wasn't the lone member of the audience. His wife was upstairs and his lawyer had helped him with his will and "theatrical" and "melodrama" imply an awareness of the effect on others, an interpersonal component, even though he was clearly being driven to suicide by the pain of his depressive disease. At the other end of the scale, borderline patients may have some real and severe distress, may be aware of this and aware of the interpersonal implications of their behavior at the same time, and yet be following an interpersonal imperative that goes beyond questions of conscious versus not conscious.

Throughout the text other cautions have been mentioned. They are worth repeating briefly here. This model is not to be used as an excuse to reject or to punish. On the contrary, properly used it should prevent the inevitable reenactment of punishment and rejection that often comes at the end of a more traditional "psycho-therapeutic" approach. And it is certainly not meant to blame the victim. But it is meant to prevent the excessive smothering care, control, and protection that at best are condescending and at worst very damaging.

The model cannot be used as a simple rote series of cookbook techniques. A therapist doing this without also understanding the model and without doing the internal work necessary is liable to jump from a position of concern, empathy, and anxiety straight through care, interest, and friendliness to hostility, punishment, and rejection. The model can be misused to justify the mental health worker's acting out. We truly hope a careful reading of this book will decrease rather than increase this possibility.

# 13

## Case Studies

In this chapter we have transcribed verbatim four case vignettes that were presented by a clinical service to a panel of visiting consultants. Part i of each case is the presentation. Part ii is a brief discussion of missing information, underlying assumptions and models, and the effect of the language used. Part iii consists of a translation of the information presented in part i into an interactional model. Part iv is the recommended plan of treatment according to relationship management principles.

### CASE I

#### i.  As Presented

The patient is a 27-year-old woman, diagnosed as borderline personality disorder, admitted from the emergency department following an overdose of prescribed medication. The overdose followed termination of a 4-month relationship with a boyfriend. Treatment was centered on stabilizing her, with particular regard to suicidal impulses. After 3 weeks of hospitalization, she shows minor improvement only.

Staff are becoming impatient with her demands for nearly constant and immediate attention. The team is meeting, and the patient interrupts the team meeting, loudly demanding that she be given an immediate interview. Staff direct her away from the meeting room, but she continues to become more physically aggressive, and again interrupts the meeting. She is sent back to her room.

Again she interrupts the meeting. The patient's therapist responds by loudly telling the patient to return to her room. The therapist then physically turns the patient around and forcibly moves her out the door of the team room, and continues to push the patient down the hall into her room. The patient quiets down, and lies on her bed calmly until she is seen later to address her concerns. The therapist feels bad. The treatment team becomes split; some complain among themselves and to their supervisor that the therapist acted improperly.

## ii. Problems in This Presentation

In the first paragraph, assumptions of cause and effect and a mechanical medical model prevent a more useful understanding of these events. How, where, with whom, in what circumstances, did she take the overdose, and how did she get to the emergency department? What happened there? Her overdose is a social event, not a private, intrapsychically driven event. We need to know the play, the interpersonal drama being acted on our stage. This is a negotiation between patient and boyfriend becoming a negotiation between patient and hospital staff. The words "stabilizing" and "suicidal impulses" reveal some kind of belief that this is a problem in her head, some kind of instability in her internal suicide control mechanisms, and that we are responsible to return this mechanism to stability. Because of the overlay of affect, responsibility, the blind adherence to the social contract of the medical model, nobody has questioned that a 27-year-old intelligent woman needs to be hospitalized because her boyfriend of 4 months broke up with her.

The second paragraph has more detailed interaction between patient and staff. The first line, however, could be misleading. The staff are probably interpreting her behavior as "attention seeking," which implies in turn a simple motivation of satisfying excessive dependency needs. This simple interpretation is never helpful with borderline patients. A display of "attention-seeking behavior" may represent either a felt need or an interactional ploy, a vehicle for engaging the staff in a dialogue about worth and control (or both).

### iii. Translation

Despite the missing information and misleading language, this scenario can be examined from a relationship management perspective. The patient is engaged in a tumultuous negotiation with the staff. Undoubtedly, she was engaged in similar negotiations with her boyfriend, and possibly with a therapist before being readmitted. One of the parameters being negotiated may be love or worth. Am I lovable, worthwhile? But the way the action unfolds with physical aggression indicates control is also being negotiated. Am I in control? Are you in control?

So far the action has followed the script. The patient says that she is not lovable and not in control of herself. The staff says that she is lovable and can control herself (the corollary of which is that they are loving and are in control). The patient puts this proposition to the test. Eventually, the therapist, responding undoubtedly to her strong sense of responsibility and the team's covert messages to the therapist to bring this patient under control, shouts at the patient and forces her to her room. This act is then complete. The therapist has now, by her actions, agreed with the patient's proposition that she is not lovable and is incapable of controlling herself. The therapist feels badly because she has been put in the position of being hateful and controlling, and has failed as a therapist.

At this point, the patient does quiet down, but at what cost? She is a reprimanded and punished child. The therapist is a guilty, hostile, rejecting, and failed parent. The curtain is about to go up on the second act.

### iv. Action Plan

She probably should not have been hospitalized, but a different social contract can still be presented to her now. In this contract she can stay for a while or leave, as she wishes. If she wishes to stay, exactly how much time (how often, when) she would like with a therapist is negotiated. The therapist is clear and honest. To counter the distorted interpersonal negotiation about lovableness, the therapist must be meticulously honest about her feelings, and must do the internal work necessary to not be driven by a need to prove she is loving or caring. The therapist will hold absolutely to the agreed-upon length and time of meeting.

The social contract will contain the clause that the patient is entirely responsible for her own behavior, including self-harmful behavior. In the forging of the new social contract, it should be overtly specified what behaviors the team will ignore (e.g., going outside and shouting, pacing) and what behaviors will bring about immediate consequences. Now the problem with inpatient treatment is that the only consequence that can be applied without forcing the team into a controlling posture is discharge. So, in this case, any physically aggressive behavior or any acts of self-harm will bring about immediate discharge.

We can help this woman, and not make things worse, only if we can stay in a position of being "not in control," and if we have no need to prove we love her.

## CASE II

### i. As Presented

The patient is a 56-year-old woman who has been relatively unresponsive to treatment for severe depression following several recent deaths of relatives, complicated by problems at work associated with a new boss. The patient was brought to the hospital by a concerned relative when the patient had almost ceased to function—stopped eating, stopped going to work, and was talking of suicide. She had a lengthy history of psychiatric hospitalizations, with the current diagnosis being major depression and borderline personality disorder.

For the first period of time of inpatient treatment, the patient was given supportive psychotherapy, and a trial of several antidepressants. Her depression seemed intractable, and she appeared to somehow enjoy the protected environment of the hospital, which provided an escape from her seemingly insoluable problems. However, staff were concerned that she represented a real suicide risk.

When the decision was made with the patient to involve her family to enhance support to her, and to assist with problem solving, she became more sickly, dependent, and suicidal. In the midst of this, another patient who was severely agitated assaulted the patient. The patient reacted by complaining that the hospital ward is an unsafe place, that the assault showed that the staff were not doing their jobs; the patient demanded to be transferred to a new psychiatrist because her medication was not working. She was very specific and incisive regarding how and when staff were failing to do their jobs. The team split, with some demanding her immediate discharge, others recommending that she required several months of hospitalization.

### ii.   Problems in Presentation

To treat this problem as borderline personality disorder may be to skate on thin ice. She could well have a major refractory depression (Guscott & Grof, 1991), with the behaviors to which the staff are reacting being secondary phenomena. The presentation reflects the split. Not enough is offered about her present and past depressions (as illness) to make a diagnosis, and yet the behaviors that may be driven by interpersonal negotiation are not described in interactional detail. The suspicion that these may be in part borderline phenomena stems from her apparent enjoyment of hospitalization, the fact that she became worse when offered family support, and the manner in which she galvanized her resources to fight staff. The split among staff is suspicious also, but it is not unknown for staff to split over a severely depressed individual who is also not a likable person.

### iii.   Translation

There is undoubtedly an interpersonal negotiation taking place. This may be a primary or secondary phenomenon. If it is a secondary phenomenon, the behaviors should improve with more successful treatment for affective disorder. However, the negotiation appears to be around the parameters of competence, power, success, and failure. The patient assumes a position of helplessness, incompetence, and powerlessness. The staff try to help competently in many different ways and fail. She becomes worse. When they "fail" in a specific way, the patient in fact points this out. Her power, her competence appear to arise out of the failure of the staff. The failed staff split. Some want to try again. Some angrily want to reject the patient.

## iv. Action Plan

While the question of refractory depression should be pursued with a careful history, an investigation, and therapeutic trials, the degree to which the interpersonal negotiations, the borderline phenomena, are at work could likewise be tested with a relationship management approach. The position the staff are being put in is that of failure, incompetence. They are trying to be competent, successful. To test the borderline phenomena, the staff need simply assume a posture of failure. They should consistently and systematically, in dialogue, perhaps through a meeting between the team and the patient, tell this patient that they have failed, they don't know how to help her, they have run out of advice, pills, suggestions. (It should be noted that this is actually very close to the truth.) In this dialogue they may review with her all the failed treatments, but should always come back to the position of there being nothing else they can think of to offer. What would she like to do? This stance must be continued through the meeting and after the meeting. If she does "switch" and ask for certain things, they should be given to her if possible. If the request is impossible, she should be simply told, in a neutral fashion, that it can't be honored. In this dialogue the team is waiting for the switch, and if it comes they should go with it. If it doesn't occur, if she sinks into a more hopeless position, a more vigorous treatment of her depression should be considered.

**i. As Presented** **CASE III**

D. is a 22-year-old woman with a long-standing history of both inpatient and outpatient treatment at a number of settings. D. was raised in an abusive alcoholic family and has been involved with both adolescent and adult psychiatric systems. She presents as fragile, immature, easily overwhelmed, unable to trust, oppositional with staff (including splitting), having severe anxiety and panic symptoms, and being frequently suicidal (with two or three attempts). Since she has more recently described hearing voices, her diagnosis has been varied. She has had trouble coping in structured supportive living environments and day programs. She is often incapacitated by depression and anxiety and "can't" do even minimal tasks. Staff involved with her care increasingly feel helpless, powerless, and frustrated, which reinforces D.'s severely low self-esteem and sense of being out of control. She has very poor problem-solving and other coping skills and perceives many interactions as punitive and/or rejecting, especially from caregivers. She repeatedly talks about dying and "not being able to take it anymore" and gets little relief from pharmacotherapy, psychotherapy, or supportive or activity-oriented treatment.

**ii. Problems with the Presentation**

There is a lot missing in this presentation. Does she exhibit other psychotic symptoms? What is the nature of the "voices," and in what context does she talk of them? What are her actual cognitive abilities? Of course, even if she does have a psychotic illness and/or some cognitive limitations, a better understanding of the interactional process would help treatment and management. The presentation implies an interactional perspective, but gives no details of actual interactions, and makes assumptions about motivation and D's inner state. A detailed account of two interactional patterns would be most helpful: the manner in which she repeatedly fails in community placements and is rehospitalized, and any one typical encounter.

### iii. Translation

An interactional description would place this translation on safer ground. However, it is clear that D assumes a posture of helplessness and worthlessness. The staff repeatedly respond, fail, and feel in turn powerless and then angry. An old relationship is being endlessly re-created in which power, competence, and worth are endlessly negotiated. When there is so little data, it is helpful to examine the natural ending of the negotiation and extrapolate from there. And the end of this repeated negotiation is that D. in her extreme position of helplessness and worthlessness will have prodded the staff to extraordinary lengths to prove their competence and love. The staff fail and become hateful. D. is still worthless and helpless, but now the staff are also worthless and helpless. So ultimately, in this context, D. has shown that she is at least as worthwhile and powerful as the staff.

### iv. Action Plan

When the interactional pattern is not clear but the ending is (ending in the sense of the natural consequences of this kind of negotiation in this context), then, as a therapeutic trial and test, the therapist and team need merely but consistently and thoughtfully adopt the end position they are now fighting against. That is the position of worthlessness and helplessness. Again, after much discussion, planning, and internal work, a conference meeting with D. present should be called. At this meeting the team leader or therapist will explain to D. that they all feel they have failed to help her in any way, they just don't seem to have the necessary skills or expertise, and therefore they are turning the situation back to D., and asking her if she has any suggestions. All treatment activities could be reviewed in this way, from pharmacotherapy to community placement. D. may respond with numerous complaints and accusations. The staff must respond with contrition and agreement. They must not defend themselves in this interaction, which would be an attempt to return to a position of worth and competence. In this dialogue the staff are waiting for the switch, though it may come in unexpected and testing ways. But if there are medications or programs that will help her, it appears they will be of benefit only within a new social contract, one in which D.'s esteem and power arise from successfully assuming responsibility and not from turning the staff into failed and hateful parents.

## CASE IV

### i.  As Presented

M. is a 33-year-old woman from an extremely chaotic family of origin. Her alcoholic mother had at least six significant relationships resulting in a number of children from various unions. She threatened to kill M. on a few occasions when M. was growing up. M. experiences unresolved grief over a number of significant losses. In the past few months, M. has experienced flashbacks of early sexual abuse along with an increased urge to harm herself. She also alluded to memories of abuse by caregivers when she was shuttled between group homes and detention centers.

She has been on the unit 2 weeks and generally presents as angry, sullen, and challenging and has made several attempts to spilt staff along with vague suicidal threats.

Recent issues:

1.  In a session on Friday, when past abuse by caregivers was raised, M. got up suddenly and punched a framed picture, breaking the glass. She has been asked to reimburse the hospital.
2.  She came back from a pass Saturday P.M. saying, "I've taken a couple of Valium from home," which she later reported was six or seven, as well as brandishing martial arts weapons, which she handed over to staff. She was contracted on not taking outside meds or being destructive.

3. She stayed out overnight Sunday (AWOL) and slept in the emergency ward waiting room and returned in the A.M.
4. Monday, her roommate reported that M. had a knife in her sock. Staff added no weapons to the contract, and she handed it in.

She is now saying, "You want me to talk about the things that upset me, but you won't let me do or say anything. I feel trapped and you're not taking away the pain. Why should I stay?"

Question: Probing into her past and exploring her flashbacks make M. feel overwhelmed and out of control, yet her flashbacks and distress are increasing and need to be dealt with. How?

## ii. Problems with This Presentation

An assumption is made of causality between M.'s "chaotic" background and her current behavior. It would be difficult to argue that there is no connection, but the manner of presentation creates a strong empathic link between M.'s background and her current distress that mitigates against consideration of other interpretations. Indeed, her troublesome behaviors are presented without interpersonal context, as if they simply arise out of her increasing distress. There is also a hidden assumption that it would benefit M. to reexperience, talk about, and/or "deal with" her past traumatic experiences. Maybe it would. But this is clearly the staff's agenda, not M.'s. The details of the contract are not given, but we might assume it to be the standard type, namely, "I promise to talk about my distress before breaking anything or taking overdoses." This is not the kind of contract we recommend.

Some of her statements are quoted verbatim but not put in context. They represent only one side of an ongoing dialogue. It would be useful to hear the other side.

### iii. Translation

The interpersonal negotiation in this case appears to be around the issues of control and responsibility. At the same time, the client might also be posing the question, "Am I lovable?" and testing the staff's increasingly ambivalent answers. The natural consequences of these negotiations include staff assuming total control (client not competent, not "able" to control herself, staff in control for the moment but have also failed as therapists) and/or discharging client ("You were right. You are not lovable and we are not loving").

A more detailed description of a typical transaction would help us decide if the dominant issue is control or if it is lovableness (worth).

M. is clear about the control issue: *"You* want me to talk . . ." The problem is owned by the staff. Treatment is their agenda and responsibility. M says quite directly that she will use this as a vehicle for negotiating her relative sense of power and control.

### iv. Action Plan

It would be nice to be able to help M. "deal with" her past, and it would be nice if this were to help her in the present and future. But this cannot be accomplished within the current distorted interpersonal transactions. To correct this, the staff (ideally the inpatient team and her outpatient therapist and/or psychiatrist) should simply meet with M. and present her with a new social contract utilizing the style and techniques described in this book. The new social contract will include the following points:

- Whether you stay in the hospital or leave is entirely up to you. We don't know what is best for you.
- What you do and what you talk about while in the hospital are also entirely up to you. You don't have to talk with anyone about past experiences unless you want to. We'd like to be able to help you. We're not sure how. You tell us what helps, with whom you would like to talk, and about what.

- You are voluntary and may come and go as you please as long as you tell us when to expect you back.
- In return we are imposing a few very straightforward rules: If you engage in any violent or destructive behavior, you will be immediately discharged. If property is damaged, you will be sent a bill. If the violence is toward a person, you will be discharged and charged with assault. If you overdose, abuse medication, or bring drugs or weapons into the hospital, you will be immediately discharged. If you leave the hospital and aren't back by midnight and don't let us know, we will immediately discharge you.

It feels incomplete to end the book at this point without some grand summarizing statements or a wise epilogue. Have we been clear enough? Have we said everything we wished to say? Maybe one more example will really get these ideas across.

But no. As the model prescribes, it is time to let go. You may reject, adopt, or improve upon all or some of the ideas expressed in this book. It's up to you.

# References

Aarkrog, T. (1981). The borderline concept in childhood, adolescence and adulthood: Borderline adolescents in psychiatric treatment and 5 years later. *Acta Psychiatrica Scandinavica, 293(Suppl.),* 1–300.

Adler, G. (1973). Hospital treatment of borderline patients. *American Journal of Psychiatry, 130,* 32–36.

Akhtar, S., Byrne, J.P., Doghramji, K. (1986). The demographic profile of borderline personality disorder. *Journal of Clinical Psychiatry, 47,* 196–198.

Akiskal, H. S. (1981). Subaffective disorders: Dysthymic, cyclothymic and bipolar II disorders in the "borderline" realm. *Psychiatric Clinics of North America, 4,* 25–46.

American Psychiatric Association. (1980). *Diagnostic and statistical manual of mental disorders (3rd ed.)* Washington, DC: Author.

American Psychiatric Association. (1987). *Diagnostic and statistical manual of mental disorders (3rd ed.—rev.).* Washington, DC: Author.

Andrulonis, P. A., Glueck, B. C., Stroebel, C. F. et al. (1981). Organic brain dysfunction and the borderline syndrome. *Psychiatric Clinics of North America, 4,* 47–66.

Aronson, T. A. (1985). Historical perspectives on the borderline concept: A review and critique. *Psychiatry, 48,* 209–222.

Aronson, T. A. (1989). A critical review of psychotherapeutic treatments of the borderline personality: Historical trends and future directions. *Journal of Nervous and Mental Disease, 177,* 511–528.

Bemporad, J. R., Smith, H. F., Hanson, G., & Cicchetti, D. (1982). Borderline syndromes in childhood: Criteria for diagnosis. *American Journal of Psychiatry, 139,* 596–602.

Blumenthal, S. J. (1990). Youth suicide: Risk factors, assessment and treatment of adolescent and young adult suicidal patients. *Psychiatric Clinics of North America, 13,* 511–556.

Bradley, S. J. (1979). The relationship of early maternal separation to borderline personality in children and adolescents: A pilot study. *American Journal of Psychiatry, 136,* 424–426.

Bradley, S. J. (1981). The borderline diagnosis in children and adolescents. *Child Psychiatry and Human Development, 12,* 121–127.

Brooks, B. (1982). Familial influences in father-daughter incest. *Journal of Psychiatric Treatment and Evaluation, 4,* 117–124.

Bryer, J. B., Nelson, B. A., Miller, J. B., et al. (1987). Childhood sexual and physical abuse as factors in adult psychiatric illness. *American Journal of Psychiatry, 144,* 1426–1430.

Buie, D. H., & Adler, G. (1982–1983). Definitive treatment of the borderline personality. *International Journal of Psychoanalytic Psychotherapy, 9,* 51–87.

Byrne, C. P., Velamoor, V. R., Cernovsky, Z. Z., et al. (1990). A comparison of borderline and schizophrenic patients for childhood life events and parent-child relationships. *Canadian Journal of Psychiatry, 35,* 590–595.

Carmen, E. (H.), Rieker, P. P., & Mills, T. (1984). Victims of violence and psychiatric illness. *American Journal of Psychiatry, 141,* 378–383.

Coccaro, E. F., Siever, L. J., Klar, H.M., et al. (1989). Serotonergic studies in patients with affective and personality disorders: Correlates with suicidal and impulsive behavior. *Archives of General Psychiatry, 46,* 587–599.

Cowdry, R. W., Pickar, D., & Davies, R. (1985–86). Symptoms and EEG findings in the borderline syndrome. *International Journal of Psychiatry in Medicine, 15,* 201–211.

Davis, G. C., & Akiskal, H. S. (1986). Descriptive, biological and theoretical aspects of borderline personality disorder. *Hospital and Community Psychiatry, 37,* 685–691.

Dawson, D. F. (1988). Treatment of the borderline patient, relationship management. *Canadian Journal of Psychiatry, 33,* 370–374.

Department of Clinical Epidemiology and Biostatistics, McMaster University Health Sciences Centre. (1981). How to read clinical journals: IV. To determine etiology or causation. *Canadian Medical Association Journal, 124,* 985–990.

Descartes, R. (1949). *A discourse on method.* London: J.M. Dent and Sons Ltd.

Deutsch, H. (1942). Some forms of emotional disturbance and their relationship to schizophrenia. *Psychoanalytic Quarterly, 11,* 301–321.

Drum, P. & Lavigne, G. (1987). Extended state hospital treatment of severely impaired borderline patients. *Hospital and Community Psychiatry, 38,* 515–519.

Edelwich, J., & Brodsky A. (1991). *Sexual dilemmas for the helping professional.* New York: Brunner/Mazel.

Egan, J. (1988). Treatment of borderline conditions in adolescents. *Journal of Clinical Psychiatry, 49* (Suppl.), 32–35.

Eppel, A. B. (1988). Inpatient and day hospital treatment of the borderline: An integrated approach. *Canadian Journal of Psychiatry, 33,* 360–363.

Esman, A. H. (1989). Borderline personality disorder in adolescents: Current concepts. *Adolescent Psychiatry, 16,* 319–336.

Famularo, R., Kinscherff, R., & Fenton, T. (1991). Posttraumatic stress disorder among children clinically diagnosed as borderline personality disorder. *Journal of Nervous and Mental Disease, 179,* 428–431.

Finlayson, R., Greenland, C., Dawson, D., Blum, H., & Pitman, G. (1983). Chronic psychiatric patients in the community. *Canadian Journal of Psychiatry, 28,* 635–639.

Frank, H., & Paris, J. (1981). Recollections of family experience in borderline patients. *Archives of General Psychiatry, 38,* 1031–1034.

Friedman, H. J. (1969). Some problems of in-patient management with borderline patients. *American Journal of Psychiatry, 126,* 299–304.

Friedman, R. C., Aronoff, M.S., Clarkin, J.F., et al. (1983). History of suicidal behavior in depressed borderline inpatients. *American Journal of Psychiatry, 140,* 1023–1026.

Fyer, M.R., Frances, A.J., Sullivan, T., et al. (1988). Suicide attempts in patients with borderline personality disorder. *American Journal of Psychiatry, 145,* 737–739.

Gabbard, G. O. (1986). The treatment of the "special" patient in a psychoanalytic hospital. *International Review of Psycho-Analysis, 13,* 333–347.

Gabbard, G.O. (1989a). On 'doing nothing' in the psychoanalytic treatment of the refractory borderline patient. *International Journal of Psycho-Analysis, 70,* 527–534.

Gabbard, G. O. (1989b). Splitting in hospital treatment. *American Journal of Psychiatry, 146,* 444–451.

Gardner, D., Lucas, P. B., & Cowdry, R. W. (1987). Soft sign neurological abnormalities in borderline personality disorder and normal control subjects. *Journal of Nervous and Mental Disease, 175,* 177–180.

Gartrell, N., Herman, J., Olarte, S., et al. (1986). Psychiatrist-patient sexual contact: Results of a national survey; I: Prevalence. *American Journal of Psychiatry, 143,* 1126–1131.

Gelinas, D. J. (1983). The persisting negative effects of incest. *Psychiatry, 46,* 312–332.

George, A., & Soloff, P. H. (1986). Schizotypal symptoms in patients with borderline personality disorders. *American Journal of Psychiatry, 143,* 212–215.

Gilbertson, A. D. (1992). Sex bias in diagnosis [letter]. *Hospital and Community Psychiatry, 43,* 406–407.

Gillmor, D. (1987). *I Swear by Apollo: Dr. Ewen Cameron and the CIA–brainwashing Experiments.* Montreal: Eden Press.

Goffman, E. (1959). *The presentation of self in everyday life.* New York: Doubleday Anchor Books.

Goffman, E. (1963). *Behavior in public places: Notes on the social organization of gatherings.* Glencoe, IL: Free Press of Glencoe.

Goffman, E. (1967). *Interaction ritual: Essays on face-to-face behavior.* New York: Doubleday Anchor Books.

Goldstein, W. N. (1987). Current dynamic thinking regarding the diagnosis of the borderline patient. *American Journal of Psychotherapy, XLI,* 4–22.

Greene, L. R., Rosenkrantz, J., & Muth, D. Y. (1986). Borderline defenses and countertransference: Research findings and implications. *Psychiatry, 49,* 253–264.

Greenman, D. A., Gunderson, J. G., Cane, M., & Saltzman, P. R. (1986). An examination of the borderline diagnosis in children. *American Journal of Psychiatry, 143*, 998–1003.

Grinker Sr., R. R., & Werble, B. (Eds.). (1977). *The borderline patient*. New York: Jason Aronson.

Grinker Sr., R. R., Werble, B., & Drye., R. C. (1968). *The borderline syndrome: A behavioral study of ego-functions*. New York: Basic Books.

Groves, J. E. (1981). Current concepts in psychiatry: Borderline personality disorder. *New England Journal of Medicine, 305*, 259–262.

Gualtieri, C. T., Koriath, U., & Van Bourgondien, M. E. (1983). "Borderline" children. *Journal of Autism and Developmental Disorders, 13*, 67–72.

Gunderson, J. G., & Englund, D. W. (1981). Characterizing the families of borderlines: A review of the literature. *Psychiatric Clinics of North America, 4*, 159–168.

Gunderson, J. G. & Kolb, J. E. (1978). Discriminating features of borderline patients. *American Journal of Psychiatry, 135*, 792–796.

Gunderson, J. G., & Phillips, K. A. (1991). A current view of the interface between borderline personality disorder and depression. *American Journal of Psychiatry, 148*, 967–975.

Gunderson, J. G., & Singer, M. T. (1975). Defining borderline patients: An overview. *American Journal of Psychiatry, 132*, 1–10.

Gunderson, J. G., & Zanarini, M. C. (1987). Current overview of the borderline diagnosis. *Journal of Clinical Psychiatry, 48* (Suppl.), 5–11.

Gunderson, J. G., Kerr, J., & Englund, D. W. (1980). The families of borderlines: A comparative study. *Archives of General Psychiatry, 37*, 27–33.

Gunderson, J. G., Kolb, J. E., & Austin, V. (1981). The diagnostic interview for borderline patients. *American Journal of Psychiatry, 138*, 896–903.

Guscott, R. & Grof, P. (1991). The clinical meaning of refractory depression: A review for the clinician. *American Journal of Psychiatry, 148*, 695–704.

Haley, J. (1969). *The power tactics of Jesus Christ and other essays*. New York: Grossman Pub.

Hansell, N. (1976). *The person-in-distress: On the biosocial dynamics of adaptation*. New York: Human Sciences Press.

Hawking, S. W. (1988). *A brief history of time: From the big bang to black holes*. New York: Bantam Books.

Herman, J. L. (1986). Histories of violence in an outpatient population: An exploratory study. *American Journal of Orthopsychiatry, 56*, 137–141.

Herman, J. L., with Hirschman, L. (1981). *Father-daughter incest*. Cambridge, MA: Harvard University Press.

Herman, J. L., Perry, J. C., & van der Kolk, B. A. (1989). Childhood trauma in borderline personality disorder. *American Journal of Psychiatry, 146*, 490–495.

Hoch, P., & Polatin, P. (1949). Pseudoneurotic forms of schizophrenia. *Psychiatric Quarterly, 23*, 248–276.

Hofstadter, D. R., & Dennett, D. C. (1981). *The mind's I: Fantasies and reflections on self and soul.* New York: Basic Books.

Hudgens, R. W. (1971). The use of the term 'undiagnosed psychiatric disorder.' *British Journal of Psychiatry, 119,* 529–532.

Kaufman, J., & Zigler, E. (1987). Do abused children become abusive parents? *American Journal of Orthopsychiatry, 57,* 186–192.

Kernberg, O. F. (1966). Structural derivatives of object relationships. *International Journal of Psycho-Analysis, 47,* 236–253.

Kernberg, O. (1967). Borderline personality organization. *Journal of the American Psychoanalytic Association, 15,* 641–685.

Kernberg, O. F. (1972). Early ego integration and object relations. *Annals of the New York Academy of Sciences, 193,* 233–247.

Kernberg, O. F. (1975). *Borderline conditions and pathological narcissism.* New York: Jason Aronson.

Kernberg, O. F. (1984). *Severe personality disorders: Psychotherapeutic strategies.* New Haven: Yale University Press.

Kernberg, O. F., Goldstein, E. G., Carr, A. C., et al. (1981). Diagnosing borderline personality: A pilot study using multiple diagnostic methods. *Journal of Nervous and Mental Disease, 169,* 225–231.

Kernberg, P. F. (1990). Resolved: Borderline personality exists in children under twelve. Affirmative. *Journal of the American Academy of Child and Adolescent Psychiatry, 29,* 478–482.

Kety, S. S., Rosenthal, D., Wender, P. H., & Schulsinger, F. (1968). The types and prevalences of mental illness in the biological and adoptive families of adopted schizophrenics. In Rosenthal, D. & Kety, S. S. (Eds.), *Transmission of schizophrenia* (pp. 345–362). Oxford: Pergamon Press.

Knight, R. (1953). Borderline states. *Bulletin of the Menninger Clinic, 17,* 1–12.

Knoll, III, J. L. (1991). Hypothesis about borderline personality disorder [Letter]. *American Journal of Psychiatry, 148,* 149.

Kohut, H. (1971). *The analysis of the self; A systematic approach to the psychoanalytic treatment of narcissistic personality disorders.* New York: International Universities Press.

Kohut, H., & Wolf, E. S. (1978). The disorders of the self and their treatment: An outline. *International Journal of Psycho-Analysis, 59,* 413–425.

Kolb, J. E., & Gunderson, J. G. (1980). Diagnosing borderline patients with a semistructured interview. *Archives of General Psychiatry, 37,* 37–41.

Kotila, L., & Lönnqvist, J. (1987). Adolescents who make suicide attempts repeatedly. *Acta Psychiatrica Scandinavica, 76,* 386–393.

Kroll, J., Carey, K., Sines, L., & Roth, M. (1982). Are there borderlines in Britain? A cross-validation of U.S. findings. *Archives of General Psychiatry, 39,* 60–63.

Kullgren, G. (1988). Factors associated with completed suicide in borderline personality disorder. *Journal of Nervous and Mental Disease, 176,* 40–44.

Lerner, H. D, Sugarman, A., & Gaughran, J. (1981). Borderline and schizophrenic patients: A comparative study of defensive structure. *Journal of Nervous and Mental Disease, 169,* 705–711.

Liebowitz, M. R., & Klein, D. F. (1981). Interrelationship of hysteroid dysphoria and borderline personality disorder. *Psychiatric Clinics of North America, 4,* 67–87.

Links, P. S. (1991). Genetic aspects of borderline personality disorder. Presentation at symposium on Borderline Personality Disorder: Building a New Understanding, Hamilton, Ontario.

Links, P. S., & Munroe Blum, H. (1990). Family environment and borderline personality disorder: Development of etiologic models. In P. S. Links (Ed.), *Family environment and borderline personality disorder* (pp. 3–24). Washington, DC: American Psychiatric Press.

Links, P. S., Steiner, M., Offord, D. R., et al. (1988). Characteristics of borderline personality disorder: A Canadian study. *Canadian Journal of Psychiatry, 33,* 336–340.

Lofgren, D. P., Bemporad, J., King, J., et al. (1991). A prospective follow-up study of so-called borderline children. *American Journal of Psychiatry, 148,* 1541–1547.

Lonie, I. (1985). From Humpty-Dumpty to Rapunzel: Theoretical formulations concerning borderline personality disorder. *Australian and New Zealand Journal of Psychiatry, 19,* 372–381.

Loranger, A. W., Oldham, J. H., & Tulis, E. H. (1982). Familial transmission of DSM-III borderline personality disorder. *Archives of General Psychiatry, 39,* 795–799.

Ludolph, P. S., Westen, D., Misle, B., et al. (1990). The borderline diagnosis in adolescents: Symptoms and developmental history. *American Journal of Psychiatry, 147,* 470–476.

Macaskill, N. D., & Macaskill, A. (1981). The use of the term 'borderline patient' by Scottish psychiatrists: A preliminary survey. *British Journal of Psychiatry, 139,* 397–399.

Macaskill, N. D. and Macaskill, A. (1985). The use of the term 'borderline patient' by Scottish psychiatrists: II. Conceptual and descriptive analysis. *International Journal of Social Psychiatry, 31,* 47–53.

Mack, J. E. (1975). Borderline states: An historical perspective. In J. E. Mack (Ed)., *Borderline states in psychiatry* (pp. 1–27). New York: Grune and Stratton.

Mahler, M. S. (1971). A study of the separation-individuation process: And its possible application to borderline phenomena in the psychoanalytic situation. *Psychoanalytic Study of the Child, 26,* 403–424.

Mahler, M. S. (1972). On the first three subphases of the separation-individuation process. *International Journal of Psycho-Analysis, 53,* 333–338.

Mahler, M., & Kaplan, L. (1977). Developmental aspects in the assessment of narcissistic and so-called borderline personalities. In P. Hartocollis (Ed.), *Borderline personality disorders: The concept, the syndrome, the patient* (pp. 71–86). New York: International Universities Press.

Mahler, M. S., Pine, F., & Bergman, A. (1975). *The psychological birth of the human infant: Symbiosis and individuation.* New York: Basic Books.

Main, T. F. (1957). The ailment. *British Journal of Medical Psychology.* 129–145.

Management of borderline personality disorders [Editorial]. (1986). *Lancet, 2,* 846–847.

Masterson, J. F. (1971). Treatment of the adolescent with borderline syndrome: A problem in separation-individuation. *Bulletin of the Menninger Clinic, 35,* 5–18.

Masterson, J. F. (1981). *The narcissistic and borderline disorders: An integrated developmental approach.* New York: Brunner/Mazel.

Masterson, J. F., & Rinsley, D. B. (1975). The borderline syndrome: The role of the mother in the genesis and psychic structure of the borderline personality. *International Journal of Psycho-Analysis, 56,* 163–177.

Mattes, J. A. (1982). The optimal length of hospitalization for psychiatric patients: A review of the literature. *Hospital and Community Psychiatry, 33,* 824–828.

McGlashan, T. H. (1983). The borderline syndrome. II. Is it a variant of schizophrenia or affective disorder? *Archives of General Psychiatry, 40,* 1319–1323.

McGlashan, T. H. (1986). The Chestnut Lodge follow-up study. III. Long-term outcome of borderline personalities. *Archives of General Psychiatry, 43,* 20–30.

McManus, M., Brickman, A., Alessi, N. E., & Grapentine, W. L. (1984). Borderline personality in serious delinquents. *Comprehensive Psychiatry, 25,* 446–454.

Mead, G. H. (1934). *Mind, self and society: From the standpoint of a social behaviorist.* Chicago: University of Chicago Press.

Meijer, M., & Treffers, P. D. A. (1991). Borderline and schizotypal disorders in children and adolescents. *British Journal of Psychiatry, 158,* 205–212.

Mills, T., Rieker, P., & Carmen, E. (1984). Hospitalization experiences of victims of abuse. *Victimology, 9,* 436–449.

Newton, I. (1934). [Principia.] In F. Cajori (Ed.), *Sir Isaac Newton's mathematical principles of natural philosophy and his system of the world.* Translated by A. Motte. Berkeley: University of California Press.

Ogata, S. N., Silk, K. R., Goodrich, S., et al. (1990). Childhood sexual and physical abuse in adult patients with borderline personality disorder. *American Journal of Psychiatry, 147,* 1008–1013.

Paris, J., Brown, R., & Nowlis, D. (1987). Long-term follow-up of borderline patients in a general hospital. *Comprehensive Psychiatry, 28,* 530–535.

Paris, J., & Frank, H. (1989). Perceptions of parental bonding in borderline patients. *American Journal of Psychiatry, 146,* 1498–1499.

Paris, J., Nowlis, D., & Brown, R. (1989). Predictors of suicide in borderline personality disorder. *Canadian Journal of Psychiatry, 34,* 8–9.

Paris, J., & Zweig-Frank, H. (1992). A critical review of the role of childhood sexual abuse in the etiology of borderline personality disorder. *Canadian Journal of Psychiatry, 37,* 125–128.

Parsons, T. (1951). *The social system.* Glencoe, IL: Free Press of Glencoe.

Payer, L. (1990). Borderline cases: How medical practice reflects national culture. *The Sciences*, July/August, 38–42.

Pearson, C. S. (1989). *The hero within*. San Francisco: Harper.

Perry, J. C., & Klerman, G. L. (1978). The borderline patient: A comparative analysis of four sets of diagnostic criteria. *Archives of General Psychiatry, 35,* 141–150.

Petti, T. A., & Law, W. (1982). Borderline psychotic behavior in hospitalized children: Approaches to assessment and treatment. *Journal of the American Academy of Child Psychiatry, 21,* 197–202.

Petti, T. A., & Vela, R. M. (1989). Borderline disorders of childhood: An overview. *Journal of the American Academy of Child and Adolescent Psychiatry, 29,* 327–337.

Pfeffer, C. R. (1985). Self-destructive behavior in children and adolescents. *Psychiatric Clinics of North America, 8,* 215–226.

Pfeffer, C. R. (1991). Attempted suicide in children and adolescents: Causes and management. In M. Lewis (Ed.): *Child and adolescent psychiatry: A comprehensive textbook* (pp. 664–672). Baltimore: Williams and Wilkins.

Pope, Jr., H. G., Jonas J. M., Hudson, J. I., et al. (1985). An empirical study of psychosis in borderline personality disorder. *American Journal of Psychiatry, 142,* 1285–1290.

Reiser, D. E., & Levenson, H. (1984). Abuses of the borderline diagnosis: A clinical problem with teaching opportunities. *American Journal of Psychiatry, 141,* 1528–1532.

Rich, C. L. (1978). Borderline diagnoses. *American Journal of Psychiatry, 135,* 1399–1401.

Rinsley, D. B. (1980). The developmental etiology of borderline and narcissistic disorders. *Bulletin of the Menninger Clinic, 44,* 127–134.

Robson, K. S. (1991). Borderline disorders. In M. Lewis (Ed.), *Child and adolescent psychiatry: A comprehensive textbook* (pp. 731–735). Baltimore: Williams and Wilkins.

Roy, A. (1982). Risk factors for suicide in psychiatric patients. *Archives of General Psychiatry, 39,* 1089–1095.

Roy, A. (1985). Suicide and psychiatric patients. *Psychiatric Clinics of North America, 8,* 227–241.

Runeson, B., & Beskow, J. (1991). Borderline personality disorder in young Swedish suicides. *Journal of Nervous and Mental Disease, 179,* 153–156.

Rutter, M. (1988). Epidemiological approaches to developmental psychopathy. *Archives of General Psychiatry, 45,* 486–495.

Sauzier, M. (1989). Disclosure of child sexual abuse: For better or for worse. *Psychiatric Clinics of North America, 12,* 455–469.

Schaffer, N. D. (1990). Maintaining a balanced treatment approach with the borderline patient. *British Journal of Medical Psychology, 63,* 11–19.

Schmideberg, M. (1959). The borderline patient. In S. Arieti (Ed.), *American handbook of psychiatry* (pp. 398–416). New York: Basic Books.

Sederer, L. I., & Thorbeck, J. (1986). First do no harm: Short-term inpatient psychotherapy of the borderline patient. *Hospital and Community Psychiatry, 7,* 692–697.

Segal, B. M. (1988). A borderline style of functioning—the role of family, society and heredity: An overview. *Child Psychiatry and Human Development, 18,* 219–238.

Sen, A., & Butler, S. (1989). The quantum loop, where gravity and matter part company. *The Sciences,* November/December, 32–36.

Shapiro, E. R. (1978). The psychodynamics and developmental psychology of the borderline patient: A review of the literature. *American Journal of Psychiatry, 135,* 1305–1315.

Shapiro, T. (1990). Resolved: Borderline personality exists in children under twelve. Negative. *Journal of the American Academy of Child and Adolescent Psychiatry, 29,* 480–483.

Shearer, S. L., Peters, C. P., Quaytman, M. S., & Ogden, R. L. (1990). Frequency and correlates of childhood sexual and physical abuse histories in adult female borderline inpatients. *American Journal of Psychiatry, 147,* 214–216.

Silver, D. (1985). Psychodynamics and psychotherapeutic management of the self-destructive character-disordered patient. *Psychiatric Clinics of North America, 8,* 357–375.

Silver, D., Book, H. E., Hamilton, J. E., et al. (1983). The characterologically difficult patient: A hospital treatment model. *Canadian Journal of Psychiatry, 28,* 91–96.

Singer, M. T. (1977). The borderline diagnosis and psychological tests: Review and research. In Hartocollis, P. (Ed.), *Borderline personality disorders: The concept, the syndrome, the patient,* (pp. 193–212). New York: International Universities Press.

Soloff, P. H., & Millward, J, W. (1983). Developmental histories of borderline patients. *Comprehensive Psychiatry, 24,* 574–588.

Sorensen, T., & Snow, B. (1991). How children tell: The process of disclosure in child sexual abuse. *Child Welfare, LXX,* 3–15.

Spitzer, R. L., Endicott, J., & Gibbon, M. (1979). Crossing the border into borderline personality and borderline schizophrenia: The development of criteria. *Archives of General Psychiatry, 36,* 17–24.

Steiner, M., Links, P. S., & Korzekwa, M. (1988). Biological markers in borderline personality disorders: An overview. *Canadian Journal of Psychiatry, 33,* 350–354.

Stern, A. (1938). Psychoanalytic investigation of and therapy in the border line group of neuroses. *Psychoanalytic Quarterly, 7,* 467–489.

Stolorow, R. D., Brandchaft, B., & Atwood, G. E. (1987). *Psychoanalytic treatment: An intersubjective approach.* Hillsdale, NJ: Analytic Press.

Stone, M. H. (1979). Contemporary shift of the borderline concept from a subschizophrenic disorder to a subaffective disorder. *Psychiatric Clinics of North America, 2,* 577–594.

Stone, M. H. (1980). *The borderline syndromes: Constitution, personality and adaptation.* New York: McGraw-Hill.

Stone, M. H. (1981). Borderline syndromes: A consideration of subtypes and an overview, directions for research. *Psychiatric Clinics of North America, 4,* 3–24.

Stone, M. H. (1989). Long-term follow-up of narcissistic/borderline patients. *Psychiatric Clinics of North America, 12,* 621–641.

Stone, M. H. (1990a). Treatment of borderline patients: A pragmatic approach. *Psychiatric Clinics of North America, 13,* 265–285.

Stone, M. H. (1990b). *The fate of borderline patients: Successful outcome and psychiatric practice.* New York: Guilford Press.

Stone, M. H. (1992). Suicide in borderline and other adolescents. *Adolescent Psychiatry, 18,* 289–305.

Stone, M. H., Hurt, S. W., & Stone, D. K. (1987a). The P.I.-500: Long-term follow-up of borderline inpatients meeting DSM-III criteria. I. Global outcome. *Journal of Personality Disorders, 1,* 291–298.

Stone, M. H., Stone, D. K., & Hurt, S. W. (1987b). Natural history of borderline patients treated by intensive hospitalization. *Psychiatric Clinics of North America, 10,* 185–206.

Styron, W. (1990). *Darkness visible: A memoir of madness.* New York: Random House.

Sullivan, H. S. (1940-1953). *Conceptions of modern psychiatry: The first William Alanson White memorial lectures* (2nd ed.). New York: W.W. Norton.

Sullivan, H. S. (1950). The illusion of personal individuality. *Psychiatry, 13,* 317–332.

Sullivan, H. S. (1953). *The interpersonal theory of psychiatry.* New York: W.W. Norton.

Sullivan, H. S. (1964). *The fusion of psychiatry and social science.* New York: W.W. Norton.

Tarnopolsky, A., & Berelowitz, M. (1984). 'Borderline personality': Diagnostic attitudes at the Maudsley Hospital. *British Journal of Psychiatry, 144,* 364–369.

Tarnopolsky, A., & Berelowitz, M. (1987). Borderline personality: A review of recent research. *British Journal of Psychiatry, 151,* 724–734.

Terr, L. C. (1991). Childhood traumas: An outline and overview. *American Journal of Psychiatry, 148,* 10–20.

Torgersen, S. (1984). Genetic and nosological aspects of schizotypal and borderline personality disorders: A twin study. *Archives of General Psychiatry, 41,* 546–554.

Tucker, L., Bauer, S. F., Wagner, S., et al. (1987). Long-term hospital treatment of borderline patients: A descriptive outcome study. *American Journal of Psychiatry, 144,* 1443–1448.

Waldinger, R. J. (1987). Intensive psychodynamic therapy with borderline patients: An overview. *American Journal of Psychiatry, 144,* 267–274.

Walsh, F. (1977). Family study 1976: 14 new borderline cases. In R. R. Grinker Sr. & B. Werble (Eds.), *The borderline patient* (pp. 158–177). New York: Jason Aronson.

Wenning, K. (1990). Borderline children: A closer look at diagnosis and treatment. *American Journal of Orthopsychiatry, 60,* 225–232.

Westen, D. (1990). Towards a revised theory of borderline object relations: Contributions of empirical research. *International Journal of Psycho-Analysis, 71,* 661–693.

Westen, D., Ludolph, P., Misle, B. A., et al. (1990). Physical and sexual abuse in adolescent girls with borderline personality disorder. *American Journal of Orthopsychiatry, 60,* 55–66.

Widiger, T. A., & Frances, A. J. (1989). Epidemiology, diagnosis and comorbidity of borderline personality disorder. In A. Tasman, R. E. Hales, & A. J. Frances (Eds.), *Review of psychiatry, 8,* 8–24; Washington, DC: American Psychiatric Press.

Widiger, T. A., Frances, A., Warner, L., et al. (1986). Diagnostic criteria for the borderline and schizotypal personality disorders. *Journal of Abnormal Psychology, 95,* 43–51.

Widiger, T. A., & Weissman, M. M. (1991). Epidemiology of borderline personality disorder. *Hospital and Community Psychiatry, 42,* 1015–1021.

Winchel, R. M., & Stanley, M. (1991). Self-injurious behavior: A review of the behavior and biology of self-mutilation. *American Journal of Psychiatry, 148,* 306–317.

Winnicott, D. W. (1955). The depressive position in normal emotional development. *British Journal of Medical Psychology, 28,* 89–100.

Wishnie, H. A. (1975). Inpatient therapy with borderline patients. In J. E. Mack (Ed.), *Borderline states in psychiatry* (pp. 41–62). New York: Grune and Stratton.

Wong, N. (1980). Borderline and narcissistic disorders: A selective overview. *Bulletin of the Menninger Clinic, 44,* 101–126.

World Health Organization. (1978). *Mental disorders: Glossary and guide to their classification in accordance with the ninth revision of the international classification of diseases.* Geneva: World Health Organization.

Zanarini, M. C., Gunderson, J. G., Marino, M. F., et al. (1989). Childhood experiences of borderline patients. *Comprehensive Psychiatry, 30,* 18–25.

Zetzel, E. R. (1968). The so-called good hysteric. *International Journal of Psycho-Analysis, 49,* 256–260.

Zilboorg, G. (1941). Ambulatory schizophrenias. *Psychiatry, 4,* 149–155.

Zukav, G. (1979). *The dancing Wu Li masters: An overview of the new physics.* London: Rider & Co.

Zweig-Frank, H., & Paris, J. (1991). Parents' emotional neglect and overprotection according to the recollections of patients with borderline personality disorder. *American Journal of Psychiatry, 148,* 648–651.

# Name Index

# Subject Index

Abuse
  alcohol, 120, 166–167, 176
  drug, 120, 166, 176
  physical, 17–20, 24, 25, 49–50,
    151–154
  sexual, 17–20, 23, 24, 25, 49–50,
    64, 133, 151–155, 187–190
  substance, 121
Acting out, definition of, 56, 146
Action plan, 181–182, 184, 186–187,
  189–190
Adolescent patients, etiology among,
  23–24
Adolescents, borderline behavior in,
  141–162
Adoption, 23
Adults, patients as responsible,
  intelligent, 93–94, 97–100, 119,
  130, 132, 147–149, 150–151
Affect, incongruity between situation
  and, 78
Affective disorder(s), 9, 11, 145
Alcohol abuse, 120, 166–167, 176
Alcoholics Anonymous, 120
Allen Institute, 63
All not as it appears to be, 67–69
Ambulatory schizophrenia, 4
American Psychiatric Association, 8,
  19
  Task Force on Nomenclature and
    Statistics of, 7, 8
American Psychoanalytic Association,
  5
Analysis, interactional/interpersonal,
  70–76, 164–167, 181, 183–184,
  186, 189

Anticonvulsant medication, 108
Antidepressant medication, 156
Antisocial personality disorder, 18
Anxiety attacks, 134–135
Appearances, 67–69
*Archives of General Psychiatry,* 9
As if personality, 5
Asking about suicide ideation,
  injunction against, 123
Assessment, of institutional context,
  74
Assigned attributes, *see* Contrary
  position
Assumption of immediate
  relationship, 79
Attention-deficit hyperactivity
  disorder, 16
Attention seeking behavior, 180
Avoidance of hospitalization, 60–63,
  83, 87–92

Behavior
  attention seeking, 180
  borderline, in adolescents, 141–162
Biological level of organization, 135,
  136
Biologic origins, 15–16
Bipolar disease, 16, 18
Borderland schizophrenia, 4
Borderline behavior, in adolescents,
  141–162
Borderline concept, history of,
  3–11
Borderline patient(s), 5, 6–7, 8, 9, 10;
  *see also* Client(s)
  as adults, *see* Adults

206